An Island of English
Teaching ESL in Chinatown

D1236081

Danling Fu

HEINEMANN
Portsmouth, NH

Heinemann
361 Hanover Street
Portsmouth, NH 03801–3912
www.heinemann.com

Offices and agents throughout the world

© 2003 by Danling Fu

Library of Congress Cataloging-in-Publication Data
Fu, Danling.
An island of English : teaching ESL in Chinatown / Danling Fu.
    p. cm.
Includes bibliographical references and index.
ISBN 0-325-00481-1 (acid-free paper)
1. English language—Study and teaching—Chinese speakers. 2. English language—Study and teaching—New York (State)—New York. 3. Chinese Americans—New York (State)—New York. 4. Chinatown (New York, N.Y.)—Social conditions. 5. Middle schools—New York (State)—New York. 6. Chinese—New York (State)—New York. 7. Fu, Danling. I. Title.
PE1130.C4F78 2003
428'.071'07471—dc21   2003005469

Editor: Thomas Newkirk
Production: Elizabeth Valway
Chapter opener calligraphy by Su Zheng. The characters translate as "struggling, learning, growing, prosperous."
Cover design: Suzanne Heiser, Night & Day Design
Cover photo: John Natuzzi
Composition: TechBooks
Manufacturing: Steve Bernier

Printed in the United States of America on acid-free paper
12 11 10   VP   6 7 8

An Island of English

Sovereignty of the people

人民有權力參加投票在 把票箱選出 也起.

To Xiaodi, and all new immigrant children who followed their parents to this country, and are continuing their dreams.

Contents

Figures

Acknowledgments

Different from my first book, "*My Trouble Is My English*," which was the product of my doctoral research and represented my growth in the context of a doctoral program, this book illustrates my learning and growth in an urban public school community, a very real and challenging world. This community is truly a diverse village with a common vision and commitment: working together to educate our children.

This book belongs to the Sun Yat Sen Middle School community, especially to all of its ESL and bilingual teachers, staff developers, and administrators. It is not just about their work, but it is indeed their work as well. Without their courage, their sincere desire to find out what is the best for their students, and their commitment for improving their school and teaching, I would never have had a chance to enter the school or any of its classrooms. My first thanks go to the faculty, the administrators, and all of the children in this community. I thank them for inviting me to their school and classrooms, for providing me with such invaluable experiences to learn about teaching the children who are not prepared for American schools, and for tolerating and experimenting with my suggestions, of which even I was sometimes unsure.

Many ESL and bilingual teachers, along with the principal and assistant principals, Alice Young, Jane Lehrach, and Pam Chin, continued to support me throughout the process of writing this book. The teachers let me walk into their rooms any time I chose to observe, to read the students' work, and to conduct interviews. Many had to give up their preparation or lunchtime for my interviews or to help collect extra data. Pam continued to schedule my research visits, contacted the teachers I had to interview, and asked the students and their parents for permission to use their work. Alice, Pam, and Jane and teachers like Ourania Pantazatos, John Lo, Shirley Yang, and Jian Zhou read chapters and gave suggestions for revision. This book is about our collaborative work and also is produced through our ongoing collaboration. The contributions that Alice, Jane, and Pam each made to my work deserve more space and are detailed in the introduction.

I also owe a great deal to George Miller, the assistant to the superintendent and a former Chinatown school principal. During the five years of my work in IS 131, he also became my mentor and a dear friend who supported, encouraged, and advised me whenever I needed him. It was he who asked me to branch out to other Chinatown schools after my four-year work in IS 131 and brought me to meet the principals in other Chinatown schools. He not only nurtured me but also pushed me to take risks.

I give my deep appreciation, to the administrators, Marguerite Staus, Amy Hom, Daria Ridney, Victor Montanez, and GinGee Moy; the staff developers, Susan Stires, Ann Powers, Maureen Kerr, Pat Lynch, and Adriana LaRaja; and the faculty in PS 1, PS 126, and PS 2, where I worked and continue to work. Their intelligence and knowledge, commitment to their profession and children, passion for learning and teaching, and seemingly never-ending energy have not only inspired me but also enlightened me to see the hope at this most frustrating period in American public education, when the standards and tests, rather than children, are threatening to take control of all instruction.

My special thanks also go to Shelley Harwayne, the current superintendent of New York School District II. She first persuaded the former superintendent, Anthony Alvarado, to bring me to the school district and later hired me to work in more Chinatown schools after my work in IS 131. It was her strong leadership, her support, and her trust in me that encouraged me and also bestowed a resilient resolve in my work. Without her clear vision for New York children and teachers, I wouldn't have continued my work in New York City.

I am indebted to Susan Stires, a dear friend and colleague, whose research on Chinese new immigrant children inspired me to see more depth in young children's second language development and whose sensitive ways of working with teachers showed me how to improve my consulting skills. Moreover, through her connection with the Chinese community in Chinatown, I became friends with a new immigrant family that has brought me deep into the community. Without Susan's help, I would still be an outsider of the Chinatown community.

It is beyond words for me to express my thanks to Yong chun Ma, Xijian He, and Richard He, a Chinatown family who have adopted me, provided me a shelter in their tightened apartment, and served me the food I can't get even in Chinatown during my visits in New York City in the past three years. They have provided me with firsthand information of how new immigrants like them struggle to make a living in this new land. I am educated, humbled, and modified by what I have seen and heard about their lives.

Maureen Barbieri, a close friend and colleague, made the birth of this book possible. She brought me to New York, coached (sheltered and fed) me through my first year, and has continued to mentor me through the years I have been working in the Chinatown schools. It was originally her idea and inspiration to write a book about our work in Sun Yat Sen Middle School, and we proposed our collaborated project and each wrote our chapters. But it turned out we each had too much to say and had to have our own separate books. During my writing, she read each chapter I wrote and gave both enthusiastic and constructive responses. Her book, *"Change My Life Forever,"* which was published a year earlier, inspired my work. I can never thank her enough.

Tom Newkirk, my former professor and the editor of my first book, is again the editor of this book. When I didn't know which direction I should take for my writing, he flew to New York to meet me, to visit the school and community I would write about, and to give me suggestions and encouragement. He didn't have to be verbose. Only a few of his words would enlighten me and point me on the right path.

Nancy Shelton, a dear friend, a colleague, and the first reader of all my writing in the past two years, has contributed to this writing more than anyone else. Her combined perspective of a researcher and a classroom teacher, her straightforward comments, and her strong sense of the English language have made me reread my work, reorganize my thoughts, and rework my language. I thank her not just for her critical reading but also for appreciating my voice. She knew when to clean my accent and how to protect my voice. Also, her prompt response to each chapter despite her own overpacked schedule has helped me complete this work on time.

My thanks also go to my dear friends and University of Florida colleagues, Linda Lamme, Zhihui Fang, and Jane Townsend, and a close community formed by my doctoral students and teaching assistants, Xenia Hadjioannou, Jirapon Dhanarattigannon, Marylou Moutash, Kate Kiss, Takako Ueno, Ivy Hsieh, and Stephanie Lytle, for our continuous collaboration, regular meetings for academic and social get-togethers, and mutual support in teaching and research. Their companionship and camaraderie have not only constantly ignited my thinking but also made any hard work both endurable and enjoyable. They each add great meaning to my work and my life.

Special credits should go to the Sabbatical Award Committee of the University of Florida. Without a semester leave from teaching responsibilities, it would have been impossible to produce this amount of work within the set schedule. I am grateful to Elizabeth Valway, my production editor, and Eric Chalek, my editorial assistant, for their professionalism and prompt pushing and advice during the production process.

My American families, the Medfords and the Jarvises, always deserve special credit for whatever I have accomplished in this country. The support, care, and love they have given to me and my son in the past seventeen years have provided us a sense of home and security and added great meaning and joy to our lives in our adopted homeland.

Last but not least, thanks to my dear son, Xiaodi, who is not only the joy and center of my life but also the constant inspiration for my professional growth. From him, I learned firsthand how a child learns a new language, adjusts to a new culture, and adapts to a new environment. After his near-fatal accident, he also showed me how a student with learning disabilities struggles to learn and survive in our educational system. His never-giving-up spirit and resilient ability have once again inspired me to see the possibility and potential of the human mind when we nurture and push it properly. Xiaodi is also the first copy editor of my writing. With his extensive vocabulary and natural sense of the English language, he polishes my writing and refines my expressions. Together, we have been through so much, and we continue to thrive in this American world, which has truly become our home. This book is dedicated to him.

Foreword

~~This is a book about teaching writing.~~
~~This is a book about English language learners.~~
~~This is a book about teaching immigrant children in an urban school setting.~~
~~This is a book about teacher learning and professional learning communities.~~
~~This is a book about a journey of self-discovery.~~

This is a powerful and practical book. Danling Fu writes insightfully and honestly about her five-year collaborative experience at the Sun Yat Sen Middle School, a New York City public school that enrolls primarily the children of Chinese immigrants. But this is not an easy book to describe briefly (as illustrated in the several different attempts above to begin this foreword with just such a description).

Nonetheless, let me pull a single sentence from the book that I think captures the book's important theme.

> We need to respect our children's home culture and language, but this respect should help them enter the new culture, further their education, and forge their new identity in this new world rather than simply maintain a unique culture and language.

I believe Danling provides American schools with an innovative model for developing curriculum for English language learners. This new curriculum framework focuses on developing children's knowledge of America and American society in their home language while also working to develop their English language proficiency. This is a curriculum framework that is child-centered and one that acknowledges the tensions between bilingual and immersion education while addressing those tensions by always asking, What is best for the child?

The framework builds a coherent school day plan that provides English language learners with powerful instruction, especially instruction focused on developing children's writing. This interdisciplinary model ends the sort of fragmentation that is too common in the school day experiences of all sorts of children who struggle to learn to read, write, speak, and think in substantive ways. In other words, Danling describes a school change project—one driven by teacher collaboration, reflection, and experimentation—that produced a powerful learning environment for the Chinese immigrant children that populate for Sun Yat Sen Middle School.

The central theme is that all teachers need to be and can be both English as a second language teachers and teachers of content. It provides a powerful argument for eliminating the narrow and arbitrary professional roles that stymie professional problem solving and produce school days filled with well-intended instruction but instruction that students experience as fragmented and often incoherent. All learners benefit from an integrated school day, a school day where lesson after lesson builds on children's strengths while acknowledging their differences. Lessons across the day that create a rich and supportive whole-day learning environment. We cannot address the needs of English language learners in a single class period, especially a class period almost wholly detached from the lessons offered during the remainder of the school day. Only by rethinking professional roles and responsibilities can schools achieve the sort of instruction that Danling describes. Only by studying the whole school day experiences of students will we see the problems we often create as a result of placing ourselves in narrow professional roles (I am a social studies teacher. I am an ESL teacher. I am an English language arts teacher).

The book tells the story of the hard work that Danling and the teachers did to puzzle through the competing theories of how best to teach English language learners. It tells about the difficulties of breaking out of those narrow organizational boxes. But it is also a practical book—practical both as a model for local school reform and as a sourcebook for curriculum planning and instructional delivery. This not a book that will tell the reader exactly what to teach and when, but a book that tells the reader how these teachers decided what to teach (and when). However, the multitude of lessons that are painstakingly described and the samples of children's writing that proliferate, especially in the latter half of the book, make this a potential guide for any teacher struggling with teaching English language learners to read, write, speak, and think in English.

I must also confess that when Danling approached me about writing this foreword, I was hesitant to agree because of my own limitations—I have not spent enough time working in the classrooms of teachers of English language learners nor have I read broadly enough in the literature related to this topic. Now, however, I am glad I was asked. The book opened my eyes. The book made me think hard about the issues. The book made me more sensitive to concerns I should have thought more about earlier. And the book convinced me that much of the debate about how to best respond to the instructional needs of English language learners is best addressed by asking, as Danling and the teachers did throughout this project, What are the children telling us? What are they showing us? How can we best help them?

Richard L. Allington
University of Florida

Introduction—Work of a Team for Change

It all began with an email from Maureen Barbieri, a friend from my time at the University of New Hampshire. It read, "I've moved to New York City and currently work as a staff developer in a Chinatown middle school. Our students are mostly new immigrants from China. I don't know why they all seem very sad. And they are so quiet. I wonder if it is possible for you to come to NYC to help us understand them and teach them better." Soon, communications between Maureen and me were frequent, and a few phone conversations with the principal, Alice Young, brought me to Dr. Sun Yat Sen Intermediate (now Middle) School, which, within District II, is known as IS 131. From 1997 to 2002, I worked as a monthly consultant two days a month in this middle school located in the southwest end of Chinatown, in lower Manhattan. The school consists of about 1,200 students (used to be 1,400) in grades 6 to 8, 90.4 percent of whom are on free lunch, 85 percent of whom are from China, and 34.5 percent of whom arrived in the past three years. In this school, there are about ninety staff and faculty, including paraprofessionals and resource teachers. The oval-shaped fortresslike brick building is about thirty years old. Dr. Sun Yat Sen's statue (the founding father of the Republic of China) sits in the front entrance hall, which sets a traditional and serious tone for the school, as Chinese are not used to being playful under the eyes of any authority.

I was hired by the school as a literacy consultant with an expertise in ESL and bilingual education. I was invited to help the faculty make their instruction more effective for the newly arrived Chinese immigrant children. With Maureen's recommendation, and after reading my book on the education of Southeast Asian refugee adolescents, Alice and her faculty had great expectations of me. That was very nerve-racking. I loved challenges and missed working with new immigrant students, but I was very uncertain of how much else I knew that Maureen and Alice didn't already. Maureen, a nationally known teacher-researcher, had the reputation of being one of the exemplary writing teachers in the country. And Alice, a native of New York's Chinatown, is a National Board Certified Teacher with fifteen years' teaching experience in Chinatown schools. I wondered how much of an impact I could make during my monthly two-day visits to the school, the only days I could spare from my own university work. I started my work in IS 131 with many uncertainties.

I began my first year working closely with Maureen; Alice; Jane, one of the assistant principals; two sixth-grade ESL teachers, Ourania and Hal; and a seventh-grade science teacher, Kiran. As a team, we shared our thoughts and expertise, read and searched for ideas, experimented with different strategies, and overcame many obstacles. We also challenged each other. None of us was really the expert, but each of us contributed his or her own expertise to improving our teaching for the best interest of our new immigrant students. My five years of work in IS 131 has been the most educational as well as nurturing experience for me.

Maureen guided me through my first year's work in IS 131, which was filled with challenges and experiments. She worked closely with both the teachers and the students. Without her hard work and support, my monthly two-day visits couldn't have been as effective, especially when we wanted to make constructive changes at school. She led the faculty study group, organized the reading clubs and feisty groups among the students, and pushed quality literature and a variety of writing into the classrooms. All her work had laid a solid base for my work, shook the ground, and set a direction for the school to change. My work focused on ESL and bilingual programs, which served the newly arrived immigrant students and students with limited English proficiency who failed the LAB test (the Language Assessment Battery test, required for all ESL students in New York State). I usually had to make certain recommendations based on my monthly two-day visits in the classrooms and the meetings with the faculty. Then Maureen was the one to carry the ideas through, working closely with the teachers in trying them out. My suggestions sometimes worked and sometimes didn't. We talked through our ideas all the time: when we were together at the school, on the way to or from her home to school (I stayed with her for every visit during my first year), and in repeated discussions on the phone and through numerous emails. She was fascinated by my insight from being an ESL learner and teacher and by my own first-generation Chinese immigrant experiences. Her sincere head nods and excitement gave me a lot of confidence, and her challenges and questions pushed me to think harder and broaden my views. I was more prepared for the work the second year, when Maureen left to become a principal in another middle school in New York City.

Alice was the first American-born Chinese American principal with whom I had worked so closely. Usually there exists a great gap between American-born Chinese and new immigrant Chinese, though both groups share the same cultural roots and traditions. Growing up and living in vastly different worlds have set these two groups wide apart in many ways. When Maureen first told me about Alice, I was impressed by her intelligence, strength, and courage, but I was a little bit hesitant, wondering if she would trust me, someone who had grown up and was educated in Communist China, from which her family had to escape. For my first visit, Alice and her husband picked me up at the airport at night. On the way to Maureen's place, she told me that she had read my book "*My Trouble Is My English*" and liked it very much. She was glad that I could come to work with them. I was relieved by her sincerity and eagerness to have me.

Alice was the fourth principal in five years hired at IS 131. When Alice came, nobody knew how long she could survive there. In stark contrast to the castlelike school building packed with more than fourteen hundred eleven- to thirteen-year-old students, she is so small and soft-spoken. But she can stand as a solid rock as an instructional leader devoted to quality education at her school. In my five years at IS 131, I saw how hard she worked, from 6:00 A.M. to 8:00 P.M. without a lunch break, often seven days a week, and how determined and committed she was to improve the school. Alice holds a strong belief in a child-centered way of teaching and puts the interest of the students before everything else. She reads, studies with the faculty study groups, frequently visits classrooms, and attends all classroom and school events in addition to performing the endless list of principal duties. She is knowledgeable, open, and caring. She respects good teaching and appreciates hard work, but she is not afraid to fight for change and push for improvement for the benefit of the students. Just by observing her, I have learned a lot about what makes a good leader.

Though Alice couldn't be with me during all my classroom visits, I could feel her support and wisdom while working in the classrooms or meeting with the faculty. She was my boss, and I had to report my work to her after each visit, but she never made me feel uneasy. I could just directly share what I observed, thought, or felt. She would listen, question, and give me suggestions. She nurtured me in so many ways as a professional in the past five years. When I was down, she lifted me up. When I was making too harsh of a judgment, she cooled me off. When I was frustrated or overwhelmed with difficulties, she redirected me and gave me advice and strength. When I was excited, she joined me, laughing and crying with me. She invited me to her school and made a home for me there. She was so happy and touched when she heard me talk about IS 131 as "my school" or "our school." She has made me feel part of the school, just as she does for all her faculty.

Jane and Pam, two assistant principals, worked with me most closely after Maureen left. Jane was with me the second year, and Pam, hired as a new assistant principal, worked with me these past three years. Without them, I couldn't have functioned as a monthly consultant in the school. Jane used to be and later Pam became in charge of the ESL and bilingual departments. They are like two strong arms for Alice, always willing to work hard. During my second year of work in IS 131, we did a lot of reconstructive changes in the ESL and bilingual departments. Jane was the one who pushed the change to happen, worked with the teachers closely by giving any support they asked for, and stood up for the students. I never liked confrontation. It was easy for me to avoid dealing with problems by coming and going as a monthly consultant. But Jane had to face all the resistance and obstacles in the process of making changes. She dealt with one problem after another gracefully and firmly and helped move the school along the direction we, the team, set together. Without Jane, I couldn't have survived my second year in IS 131.

In the past three years, Pam was my guide. Before my visit, Pam would work out the schedule of my classroom observations, workshops, and meetings with faculty and then inform the faculty and email me a copy. When I came, I would meet Alice and Pam in Alice's office before school started to catch up, to plan or discuss certain issues before my classroom visits. Then Pam would accompany me to my classroom visits, to the debriefing meetings with the teachers afterward, or to workshops I gave. Usually we would visit and debrief with four or five teachers a day. It would be hard for me, as a monthly consultant, to see much in any isolated lesson without Pam, especially to make recommendations based on these observations. Pam worked with the teachers on a daily basis. She not only assisted teachers to improve and implement new strategies in their teaching but also provided me with a history or a context of the lessons I observed. We talked before and after our visit to each classroom and then put our thoughts together on what worked well and what could be better at our lunch break. For three years, I relied heavily on Pam to function effectively as a monthly consultant professionally and emotionally.

As a monthly consultant, I didn't have a chance to form really close relationships with any teachers or students, as I have with Maureen, Alice, Jane, and Pam. But no doubt, I have learned the most from observing them in classrooms and from working with them in testing new ideas and strategies. As a teacher myself, I understood how hard it must be for a teacher to have someone like me, a so-called specialist, accompanied with another school authority figure, observe her teaching, check the students' work, and evaluate her teaching and make suggestions for further action. I tried hard to comfort teachers by saying that I came to figure out how to teach our children effectively. I was neither an expert nor an authority, merely a resource to help them search for better ways to teach our children. I encouraged them to take risks and experiment together with me. Anyhow, it was hard for the teachers not to see me as an inspector or a judge of their teaching. For a while, some teachers taught the way they thought I wanted and only tried the strategies I suggested when I visited their rooms. When that happened, they tended to do a poor job. I had to reconvince them not to do anything simply for me if they didn't believe it or didn't feel comfortable trying it. It took a long time for some teachers to feel comfortable with having me sit in their rooms and to believe I was not sent by the principal(s) to pick on them.

I admired the first group of teachers, Ourania, Kiran, and Hal, who volunteered to work with Maureen and me. They were truly the pioneers and had to put up with me when I myself was paddling in strange water, searching for direction. I could be very confusing sometimes. Later, many of the new young teachers bravely joined our team and willingly took risks in the most vulnerable stage of their career. Alice tried very hard to protect as well as nurture them. I have seen them maturing quickly as teachers. In my five years of work in IS 131, I had an opportunity to work with every teacher in the ESL and bilingual departments, some more and some less, and later on, with more focus on the teachers who worked with the most recently arrived immigrant students.

I was hired to work in IS 131 because of my research and work with new immigrant students, and also because of my shared background and experience with the new Chinese immigrant students who made up 85 percent of the student population. Having been a teacher for many years in China, and a new immigrant myself in this country, I thought I shared the same cultural background and living experiences and I would understand the new Chinese immigrant students with little problems. But to my surprise, it was quite a learning experience for me to work with this student population. Reading and listening to their stories opened my eyes to students I rarely confronted in my seven years of teaching in China and to a kind of Chinese immigrant with whom I was unfamiliar in this country. Though we are grouped as the same type culturally and linguistically in the United States, we differ in many ways. Knowing them and working with them has enriched me, educated me, and also helped me connect with the people with whom I share the same roots, but we have had undeniably different life experiences in both our old and new countries.

During the past three years, I came to know a few families in Chinatown who immigrated to this country recently. I stayed with one of them during my visits and became good friends with them all. They ushered me into their lives and the Chinatown community, where I was always an outsider, and helped me understand their deep feelings and everyday struggles to survive in this country. I tried to find research on this recent group of immigrants in Chinatown, but there is so little available. I searched in the community library and museum and could hardly find anything. I was told that there was a lack of research because it was hard to trace the new immigrants, who were and are trying to be invisible because of their illegal status. I was fortunate to win the trust of a few families of new immigrants in Chinatown who helped me understand them and learn more about the children's backgrounds.

In this book, I will first share what I have learned about the new Chinese immigrant children in Chinatown, New York, their family backgrounds and living conditions, and their first living experiences in their adopted homeland. I will use these children's words to tell their own stories and interviews from adults in the community as a testimony of their experiences in this new land. Many of the students' works were written in Chinese and the interviews with the Chinatown residents were all conducted in Chinese, and the English versions of their words and work in the chapters are all my translation.

The main body of the book illustrates how the teachers, administrators, and I worked together to solve problems and search for effective methods to reach the newly arrived Chinatown immigrant students. These students lack the content knowledge needed for American education, have limited to no English proficiency, have no parental or adult support at home for their school work, and need to make tremendous adjustments emotionally, socially, culturally, and academically in their new lives in America. It had been a challenge to deliver the same curriculum used for students of the same age in the United States schools to our students, who lacked so much in their education and lives. However, under the leadership of Alice, we all worked hard to make miracles.

As a consultant, I observed teaching, debriefed with teachers, read students' work, gave workshops, and made recommendations. Since I visited the school only two days a month, what I could do was very limited. It was the teachers who did all the work. To give an idea is easy, but to make it work takes a lot of effort and adjustment. From chapter to chapter, I will illustrate how we worked together schoolwide to solve major problems, one after another. As a consultant, I did make a lot of suggestions and recommendations. I will explain why I decided to make those suggestions, what worked and what didn't, and how I revised my ideas. This process resembles the writing process: I often started a draft, a rough idea, and teachers responded to it, trying to make sense out of it in reality, and then we refined it and polished it or dumped it altogether.

Sometimes, a rough and vague idea of mine could cause a lot of pain and confusion for the teachers. So they asked for demonstration lessons. I did a few demo lessons, such as how to manage small groups and use pattern books, but I never liked the idea of demo lessons from a consultant. I believe teaching is not a showcase, but a holistic process. A teacher needs to know all his or her students and the context of a lesson—its pre- and post-activities and its connection to the overall unit or curriculum. Good teaching needs constant revision and catches teachable moments. For me, as a monthly consultant, when I did demo lessons, I lacked all the important information and links and didn't have a second chance to revise the work. After each attempt, I always felt incomplete, and I wished to have a chance to make the work better. I shared my thoughts with Alice, and she understood me and rarely pushed me to do what I didn't believe in or felt uncomfortable doing.

During the five years of my work in IS 131, I took notes of classroom observations and recorded my own thoughts and comments from teachers and administrators. I interviewed teachers, students, residents, and restaurant and sweatshop workers in Chinatown. I visited the Chinatown museums and libraries and interviewed staff there. All of these notes and interviews are the basis for this book. Of course, I collected a multitude of the students' writing— drafts and published pieces. They were the most compelling evidence of our work and offered the most insightful information about our students. But unfortunately, because of my limited time at school and the nature of my work as a consultant, I didn't have the chance to see how the pieces were produced, or even get to know the individual authors. So in this book, the students' works are cited to inform about them in general rather than as individuals, to reveal their ability as thinkers and writers, to explain our work, and to show the results of our teaching. I use these students' writing samples in the chapters to illustrate various points I try to make, but not for any case studies or to show the development of an individual student's literate growth. Among them, some are the best work written by the most advanced students, and some may represent a stage of language development for a certain group of learners.

Currently, there have been some changes in using proper terms to define new language learners in the field: from ESL (English as a second language), to LEP (students with limited English proficiency), to ELL (English language learners). The reason for the change is this: for many of the "ESL" students, English may not be their second language, but rather their third or even fifth language. I was debating which term I should use to address the students I describe in this book. Finally I decided to use the term *ESL*, because all the students whom I discuss in this book are Chinese, and English is their second language. Last summer, when I went back to visit China, I shared my work in Chinatown schools at a literacy conference, and the Chinese educators showed great interest in my work. And so far, *ESL* is the only term they know and use to address English language learners. Also for this reason, I use the term *ESL* for the students I discuss in this book and for the book title as well.

Throughout the book, I share my thoughts and reflections as an educator who has understood more about teaching while helping other colleagues improve their teaching, and as a new immigrant who was pushed to examine myself while learning about the people who seemingly shared the same roots and experience as mine. All these learning experiences have made me realize how lucky I am: I have the luxury to observe others teach, to see others experiment with my ideas, and to be able to step aside from teaching to think

,er. Most of our teachers don't have this luxury. They are constantly
,, often in the middle of a mess, having to work wonders under pressure
l directions and also having to listen to the so-called specialists, like
me. onically, though hired as a specialist in ESL and bilingual education, I
learned the most about ESL and bilingual education from observing and
working with the teachers and students of IS 131, more than ever in my life.
Knowing more and more about the new immigrants in Chinatown has
enlightened and modified me at the same time. Learning about them makes
me think about my own son and me and provokes me to ponder if they will
ever have more opportunity than my son and me in this world, after they tried
so hard to leave the country where they were born with little opportunity. How
can we really help them reach their American dreams? What else should we
do for them in their schooling in addition to what we are already doing? As
an educator, I will live with these questions for a long time. This book may
conclude with more questions than answers.

The New Chinese Immigrants and Their Lives in Chinatown

Ninety-eight percent of the recently arrived Chinese immigrant children in IS 131 were from villages near Fuzhou, the capital of Fujian province, in southeastern China, across the strait from Taiwan. Those villages have a long tradition of men going abroad to make money and women taking care of the children and the elderly at home. In the past, Southeast Asia was the place for these men's fortune making. Starting at the end of the 1980s, they switched their destination to the United States because they heard about its better social system with more opportunities for new immigrants. Another big difference for men going abroad recently from those in the earlier years is that recent immigrants intend to emigrate permanently rather than going abroad simply to make money, send it back to support families, and eventually return to their homeland. Traditionally, uprooting a family was unthinkable to Chinese. Living abroad was considered treason. Now a desire to better their and their children's future has made desperate Chinese drift away from the tradition. Among these immigrants from the Fuzhou area, most of them come to the United States illegally, by paying large amounts of money to smugglers. According to the *New York Times*,

> Fujianese leaders in New York estimate that at least 300,000 Fujianese are now scattered across just about every state. Precise figures do not exist because most of the immigrants entered illegally. . . . The smuggling business still casts a shadow. Passage can cost $40,000, a crushing sum in light of the poverty of Fujian province, a mineral-rich area of farms and fishery where only 9.8 percent of the 33 million people complete high school and the average yearly income for the city dwellers is $785. (Sachs 2001, 26)

Usually the men smuggle out first and work for years to pay back the money borrowed from friends or their debt to smugglers. At the same time, they have to pay attorneys to legalize their status, which can take five to seven years. After they become legalized, they apply for their wives and children to join them in this country. It may take them eight to ten years before they can be reunited with their families.

The majority of the children in IS 131 come from this background. They were separated from at least one of the parents for years; some were left to their grandparents soon after they were born, and some of their fathers left for America even before their birth. It has been quite common among Chinese immigrants to leave their families. It is hard to move the whole family to a strange land without financial security and knowledge of the new environment. So usually men come out first by themselves, and later, their wives and children, and even their own parents, come to join them.

The length of family separation for the illegal immigrants is the longest among all the Chinese immigrants. It takes them at least seven to eight years to reunite the families. When their children finally come to join them, they encounter the most difficulties in their readjustment to family life, to schooling, and to the social environment in this new land. First, children come to join parents they barely know, having left behind all the people who took care of them since their birth. The miserable feelings of separation from their grandparents, their relatives, and their friends with whom they grew up began before they left China and remain in their lives every day in this country for a long time. In their writing, the children filled the pages with pain, loss, and grief. A seventh grader wrote in Chinese four months after her arrival in America:

> May 6, 2000 was the day I would never forget. That was the day I left for America. I was told during all my growing up that America was a beautiful country in a far way land where my parents were. It was a hard day, as I had to depart with the families I grew up with. I was also nervous to meet the parents I had no memory of.

In China, people usually don't like to move away from their hometown. "Stick to the roots" is the way Chinese prefer to live. So they are not used to separation, especially when they don't know when they will be united again with the families, loved ones, and friends they left behind. These children came to join their parents or other family members in this country, but they don't see it as a family reunion, but rather as a new life with strangers in an unfamiliar land. An eighth grader wrote:

> Walking out of the airplane felt weird
> Another part of my life was awaiting me
> A family member who was never known to me

Standing in front of me
Seeing him brought no memories
Just a blank space
There was conversation from the airport to his home
The smile on his face when he looked at me
Made me think that he liked me
The first minutes spent with him
Seemed like years.

Overwhelmed by strangeness, the children feel lonely, sad, and homesick; such feeling has dominated their daily lives:

Loneliness,
Sadness.
All from my grandmother.
I vanished from a place
That is full of sadness
"Miss you" are the only words we can say
"Lonely" is the only feeling we have
One day I will be strong enough
To bring her
To the land where I lived.

When they lived in China, they were surrounded by family members and were constantly cared for by adults. They were rarely left alone for one moment by themselves. One student said that her grandma "carried [her] on her back every day while working in and out of the house." But when they came to America, they had to live a life without adults because their parents had to work hard day and night to make ends meet. Though there is little communication between adult and child, the children could feel their parents' pain.

My Dear Father

My father works every day.
He feels tired.
But he doesn't tell us.
Most days I can't see him even once.
When he goes to work in the morning.
I am asleep.
In the night when he comes back.
I am asleep again.
I just can hear his voice in the night.
But I can't see him.
My dear father I miss you so much.

In America, these children started to live a life without adults soon after they arrived in this country, as the school staff reported: "The parents dropped the kids off the first day, and we would never see them again." The children have to take care of themselves. Very often, they leave their homes in the morning when their parents either are sound asleep or have already left for work. After school, they return to empty apartments, lock themselves in, and sit in front of the TV. Later, they feed themselves with the leftover food in the refrigerator or get dinner from McDonald's, do homework, and later go to bed. The siblings take care of each other. Every day is exactly the same. The weekend is too long for them and they cannot wait to come back to the school.

Many people in this country think these immigrant children must be so happy because they left a country of poverty and came here to "heaven." Actually, these children had a different view. First, they didn't understand why they had to come:

1997 is the year
that I hate
It had so many things
That made me sad.
January 20 was the day
I left for America.
It makes me cry to think of it.
Riding in a car
Passed [past] my school,
The place I played with friends.
I heard bells ring.
On the airplane,
Thinking about my life,
I was angry with my parents
Forcing me to come to New York.
Why did this happen to me?

They miss the happy, loving, and close family life with their relatives and grandparents. The description of what these children did with their grandparents in China makes everyone understand their pain and loss more. They miss China.

I was a baby when my mother went to America. I stayed in China with my grandmother and grandfather. I was very happy because I went with my grandparents to the hills. We sang songs going up the hills. I wish next year I can go back to China and go up to the hills with my grandparents again.

A student contrasted her lives in China and in America:

I miss China too much. I miss all my relatives, teachers, and friends, uncles, aunts, cousins and grandparents in China. There was so much to do in China: games, swimming, parks, and oceans, bicycling. When we didn't have school, we ran all over the hills and fields, so much fun. Here we are locked in-cage-like-apartment and live like caged-birds with bars on the windows, from which, all you can see was other old buildings and their barred windows.

Rolling mountains, lush hills, ripe-orange picking, flowing rivers, deep lakes, glittering fields, grazing cows, and cheerful grasshoppers were part of their old life. In contrast, in their crowded apartments in Chinatown, they felt like "caged birds." They disliked their new home, new land, and the way in which they had to live. Then why did they come? Most of the children were told that they could receive a better education and have a better future in America. A seventh grader wrote about why his family decided to move to America.

> After I was born, my father's mom who was in America asked us to come to America and start a new life. She said "Your child will get a good education and it is really a good place to live." So my mother and my father thought it through and both had the same picture in their heads of what it would be like. My mother pictured that the Americans would take care of you and have a nice environment so her child could learn and live in it.
>
> So we finally came. After a year in New York, my mother was not close in guessing what it would be like in America. The environment was filled with garbage, and the air dirty. After a few years passed, the feeling of better life in America was gone.
>
> But now my mother is believing that the better life will be the answer in the future. She always believes better things lie ahead.

Among the virtues in the Chinese culture is to sacrifice the present for the future. That is why so many people are willing to give up so much (some even risk their lives) to pursue a better life and future for their children, believing that if they work hard, this land of opportunity will bring them and their children more fortune and a better life that China couldn't provide for them. But it is hard for the children to tolerate a life with little family flavor and to live with a hope of an uncertain future.

As a new immigrant myself, I could sympathize with their pain and their grief in their new lives in this world, heard in the voices of these children. I came to this country seventeen years ago and was also separated from my family for a few years before my son and husband could join me. I experienced the same loneliness and loss in my daily life in those years. But I rarely thought from my son's perspective of how he would feel when he came to a mother he barely remembered and was put immediately in a school with all English-speaking children and teachers. When he first came, he frequently complained about a stomachache, and he often missed his father and the nanny who took care of him since his birth. He would cry on the phone when hearing their voices and weep terribly when I had to leave him with the neighbors for out-of-town conferences. But not until I read these children's writing about their pain and loss did I realize that my son might have suffered the same loneliness and loss.

Though my son suffered a similar loss as the Chinatown children, he had quite a different experience from theirs in his new settlement. When my son came to me at age seven after a separation of three and a half years, we lived in the graduate family dorm at a university in New England. As a graduate student, I could attend to him most of the time before or after school. During the days when I had afternoon classes, our Chinese graduate students organized an after-school program for these children. We took turns coaching the children in Chinese language, singing, math, and calligraphy. With one-fifth of the Chinese students' families (around thirty families) living in the dorms, my son felt pretty much at home. He had all kinds of playmates: Chinese and children of many other nationalities. He swam in the summer, skated and sledded in the winter, and was never locked in the apartment. We lived quite frugally at that time, but he didn't feel any difference from what he had in China, except he missed his family members. Moving from a big-city life in China to life in a rural area in America, he became like a little wild dog rather than a caged bird, as those Chinatown children felt about themselves. He seemed much happier and less lonely than the new immigrant children in Chinatown, New York.

A child's living environment does make a tremendous difference in his adjustment. This makes people wonder: why did all those immigrants settle in New York's Chinatown, a place considered an urban ghetto for Chinese immigrants? People would say that there are so many places in America like the villages they left in China where they could resume the life they had left, like my son and I did in New England. But there are different types of Chinese immigrants from different backgrounds, who come with different purposes and through different channels to the United States. The parents of the children that settled in New York's Chinatown had no choice but to start their first homes there. People choose to live in the "ghetto" for reasons. Will they ever leave Chinatown? Some have tried but moved back later. The people I interviewed all expressed that Chinatown was a place they felt the most comfortable.

Chinatown, a Home Away from Home to All Chinese

I always like going to Chinatown whenever I visit a city that has one. A city that has a Chinatown is always attractive to Chinese. When I lived in New England, I treated myself to a monthly visit to the Chinatown in Boston. Chinatown has different meanings to different people, even to different types of Chinese.

To non-Chinese, Chinatown is a tourist place with exotic food and strange shouting; it is like a foreign land a bus ride away. To Chinese, it is a home away from home: fresh vegetables, fruits, meat, and seafood piled along the crowded streets, fish swimming in the tank, live chickens and ducks with their heads stuck out of packed wire containers, slippery eels slivering in water, shrimp jumping up and down, and turtles with their heads tucked in their shells all make the town alive. Seeing all this just soothes our eyes, though we can't ignore the smell, the flow of bloody water, and the trash flying along the sidewalks. The roasted ducks hanging upside down, barbecued ribs, well-cooked pig ears, chicken feet, not only inspire appetites but also arouse nostalgia and a feeling of being home. The streets are crowded with vendor stands and the air is filled with delicious smells of dim sum and other delicacies. No wonder people say "Chinese can eat everything with four legs except the table."

I'll never forget the first time I visited Chinatown in Boston. I arrived in America just before the Thanksgiving holiday. My host family had a big family reunion and served a traditional American Thanksgiving feast. Among all the food, the only one I could appreciate was ham, which tasted similar to preserved pork in China. So I ate quite a lot and got really sick, throwing up all night. The sickness made me terribly homesick. Then a call came from a Chinese friend in a nearby town. He said that he was visiting Chinatown in Boston and asked if I would like to go. I jumped out of bed. Despite how weak I was, I wanted to take the trip. My host mother was worried, wondering if I was strong enough to take an hourlong ride and then walk around Chinatown. I will always remember what that trip did for me. Just by walking on the street, seeing all the familiar things, and breathing in all the home-kitchen smells, I regained my strength, had a big meal at a Chinese restaurant, and felt perfectly healthy instantly. Though Chinatown has never been that magical again, it never ceases to attract me. It is a place where I can recognize, name, and know everything, and where I can just be a Chinese, as I know how to bargain, to order, to respond appropriately without a second guess, and to present myself to different types of people. It is a place where I don't feel like I am a foreigner. But it has never occurred to me to move to Chinatown. Although I don't feel strange there, I don't identify with its residents. The Chinatown people also can tell that I don't belong there.

Chinese Immigrants, New York's Chinatown, and Its Settlers

Chinatown, New York, was established in the late 1850s, as a refuge for the early Chinese immigrants from the persecution of harsh treatment from the white settlers in the West and the Chinese Exclusion Act (1870) that forbade Chinese from many jobs in California after the completion of railway and mining construction. They came to New York one, two, and a dozen at a time from the West Coast. By 1890, the Chinese population of New York had grown to 2,259 (Wong 1982). Before 1965, Chinatown in New York was known as a "bachelor's town" because of the immigration law that forbade the Chinese from becoming citizens and placed restrictions on the immigration of Chinese. Therefore, according to the Bureau of Census statistics, out of 909 Chinese in New York State in 1880, only 12 were women. By 1890, when the Chinese population in New York State had increased to 2,935, only 33 were female. Male predominance persisted until 1965 (Wong 1982).

After 1965, when immigration laws changed for Chinese, marking the end of eighty-five years of bias against the Chinese, the Chinese immigrant population in New York rose from 33,000 to 70,000 in five years, and by 1980, it became 150,000, with an almost equal ratio between men and women: 37,504 to 31,820. Among them, 50 percent located in Chinatown and depended upon the "ethnic" businesses, for their livelihood, which were mainly restaurants, garment factories, laundries, and groceries (Kwong 1987). As a matter of fact, the Chinese did not come from a nation of launderers and restaurateurs. Rather than being a Chinese ethnic business, this type of enterprise is the product of Chinese immigrants adapting to their lives in this new world since the early days. As Wong (1982) states:

> These occupations are the result of their [the Chinese immigrants'] adaptation to the economic environment in the U.S. The Chinese who came to America in the nineteenth century were principally laborers who were engaged in railroad building, exploitation of mines, and clearance of farm lands in the western frontiers. Along the transcontinental railroad and the western frontiers, some Chinese restaurants were established, not as gourmet, luxurious enterprises, but as simple eateries to serve the Chinese laborers. Hand laundry shops were also established because there were no housewives or women to do this chore and, since laundry was always considered to be women's work, very few White men entered this trade. From the frontier days, the Chinese learned that laundry is a low capital business with no competition from other White people. With some soap, scrubbing boards, and physical labor, a person could start his own business. The hand laundry soon captured the attention of other Chinese who were discriminated against in the job market immediately after the completion of the transcontinental railroad in the 1870's. Restaurant and laundry business have since then been important ethnic enterprises for the Chinese. (37)

Among all the Chinese I know or have interviewed who work in this type of so-called Chinese ethnic business, few of them had ever engaged in this kind of work back in China.

Before 1980, the majority of the Chinese immigrants came from Taiwan, Hong Kong, and Guangdong province in Mainland China. This was because Taiwan and Hong Kong have been always open to the outside world, and Guangdong has a long tradition of emigration to the United States. The majority of early immigrants to the United States came from Guangdong (99 percent, according to Kinkead 1992), and later, after 1949, people emigrated from Taiwan and Hong Kong. The people from those three places then dominated the population in New York's Chinatown. In the late '70s and early '80s, as a result of the establishment of a relationship between the United States and the People's Republic of China in the early '70s, many people from Mainland China immigrated to the United States. First came the people who wanted to join their families and relatives whom they had been separated from for more than twenty years, since 1949 when China became Communist-governed, and later, many scholars and students came to America to advance their professions when the Chinese government decided to modernize the country.

Among the recent Chinese immigrants, there are three major types: those coming to join their families in America, those coming to pursue advanced degrees or do research in academic institutes, and those smuggled to this country. Among them, the people who don't speak English, and can only work for and live among other Chinese, choose to settle in Chinatown. Most of the Chinese smuggled to this country come from the Fuzhou area. They don't speak English and have to live in Chinatown. They can get only the jobs few people want. They work sixty to eighty hours a week (sometimes as much as fourteen hours a day and six days a week), get paid very poorly (five to eight hundred dollars a month), and live in the most inhumane conditions by American living standards (Kinkead 1992).

These people usually lived a life without many opportunities for themselves or for their children in China. They come from farming villages where they have had no chance to get into college or find stable jobs. They admire the families that regularly receive money from relatives abroad, but they don't have a chance to come out of China through any legal channels. The only way to make their dream come true is to be smuggled out. Their number one destination is America, where they are told there is the most opportunity for work. Their second choice of immigration is to Europe, or other developed countries like New Zealand, Australia, and Japan. The last on their list are the countries in Southeast Asia, Africa, and the Pacific Islands. To them, it seems any place on the earth would have better opportunities than those China could give to them. They are willing to pay anything to get out. The highest cost is to America. They borrow the money to pay part of the cost in their country, and after they get into America, they pay the rest.

As soon as they get into this country, they have to work. With so much debt to pay back, without legal status, and with the desire to become legalized and have their families join them someday, they are willing to take any jobs available. They don't mind working hard or long hours and are afraid only of not being able to find jobs. Many of them worked in farming and construction in China, where they never made much money. They are used to hard work under poor conditions. So a job in a restaurant or garment factory in New York's Chinatown doesn't sound too harsh to them, and every dollar they make is worth eight Chinese *yuan*, a day's pay in China. They are always ready to work overtime, though many times with a heavy heart and tired smile, as they want to make more money, which makes the date of reunion with their families that much closer. This dream drives them to work like an overrun machine.

They spend very little, usually sleeping on the couches of their relatives or friends. Some live in the corners of someone's unfinished basement. Some rent an apartment together, with five bunk beds in one room stacked all the way to the ceiling. Some share beds with others on two shifts: one sleeping during the day and the other at night, without ever seeing each other. They find the cheapest way to live and pay the least attention to where they sleep. Journalist Gwen Kinkead (1992) described a living situation for a group of Chinese illegal immigrant laborers in Chinatown in her book *Chinatown: A Portrait of a Closed Society* as follows:

> The place, originally a one-bedroom apartment, was dark and close-smelling. A twenty-foot-long corridor that ended in a grimy window ran along one side of it. The left wall of the corridor, made of rough, un-painted plywood, enclosed what used to be the living room. It had been subdivided by more thin plywood partitions into three bedrooms, for six people. The bedrooms had sliding plywood doors each secured with a tiny padlock, like a cabin on a ship.
>
> Lin showed me his bedroom, the compartment nearest the windows. It was seven feet by six—smaller than many closets in New York City apartments. A bunk bed took up most of the space. The top bunk had a straw mat over bright sheets. The bottom bunk was Lin's. The distance from the bed to the windows was two steps. Two people could not pass in the space.
>
> The kitchen, about five by eight, had the same air of desolation. The faucet was broken and ran incessantly—a melancholy sound. There was a small four-burner gas stove, used mostly by Lin and his bunkmate, a cloth presser in a garment shop, who was about his age. The icebox worked.

>In the bathroom, the toilet had no seat. . . . In back of the bathroom
>was the original bedroom, where four more people, one of them a smuggler
>importing Chinese from Fujian Province, lived.
>
>The place could accommodate ten people, but some of Lin's roommates
>had moved away recently, leaving seven. The man living alone in the cubi-
>cle next to Lin's paid $200 a month rent; Lin and his bunkmate paid $125
>apiece; and the four occupants of the near bedroom paid $100 each. (17–18)

By living in such a condition, these Chinese immigrants pay off their debt,
save money to legalize their status, and send money to their families in China.
They work and live like this for years until they are able to send for their
families, which can take as much as eight to fifteen years.

As a recent Chinese immigrant myself, I was shocked to hear the stories
of how these immigrants came and how they work and live in Chinatown. The
following stories of three men who came from the same hometown in the
Fuzhou area represent the typical situations of the recent Chinese immigrants
who were smuggled into this country (interviewed in June, 2001).

A small take-out Chinese restaurant owner in his late thirties

I smuggled out in 1987. When I first came, I worked in the kitchen, making five hundred dollars a month, working fourteen hours a day and six days
a week. Later, I became a cook, and made much more. It took me seven
years to pay the debt [the fee to the smugglers], about thirty thousand dollars.
Eight years later, I got my wife, son, and daughter to join me. Then we
borrowed the money from relatives and friends to buy this take-out restaurant, and it took us another three years to pay the debt. Now it is easy, as
we finally don't owe debt anymore. We work all year long, and only take
a one-day break, that is Thanksgiving. All I want is to sleep—never feel
enough—or sit together with my family to chat and watch TV. Being in this
country for fourteen years, I never visited any place, but work, work all the
time. But at least we have work to do, and can make money. In China, we
had no chance for any jobs. Farming didn't give us much. I am lucky that
all my family is together. Though work is hard, I am happy and feel hopeful
for my family.

A restaurant deliveryman in his early forties

I came to this country in 1993, that was my second time to smuggle out of
the country. The first time I was caught in Malaysia and sent back. Then I
tried later and came from Mexico, and got into the country. I have a wife and
two children in China, and couldn't get them here, because I was not granted
legal status. It is not as easy as before to become legalized. I don't know if I
will ever get my family here. If not, I will work until I retire, maybe around
sixty years old, [then] I will go back. It is hard, but I can't go back now. How

can we live without any way to make money in China? Now I send money back to the family and they live quite comfortably there. I haven't paid off my debt yet. If they come, it is easy to pay debt as my wife and I could work together. I have every Sunday off. On that day, I just sleep and watch TV.

A nineteen-year-old kitchen helper

I came here only four months ago, and almost died while climbing the cliffs at the Mexican borders. The smugglers didn't tell us about any dangers on the way, and I didn't expect it was that hard. My sister and I came together and paid one million Chinese *yuan* [about one hundred thousand dollars] to the smugglers. It will probably take five years for three of us [another sister is in Japan] to pay off my part. My sisters will get married, so their husbands can help pay off their debts. I never worked in kitchens or cooked a meal in China, and now I have to work in the restaurant kitchen, fourteen hours a day and six days a week. I make five hundred dollars a month. It is hard, but it is better than having no chance to make any money in China. Now I can have some money to send back to my parents each month. I don't know when I can go back to see my parents. I don't think that far, but live and work day by day. Some days I get depressed and sad, but what can I do? I can't go back as there is so much debt on my back. When I pay off all the debt, that is the day when I will feel so relieved.

I thought I had experienced quite a bit of hardship when I first came to this country until I heard their stories. Unlike the people smuggled to this country, I rarely worked below minimum wage, didn't have to work long hours, and didn't have to pay to legalize my status. I never lived in conditions like theirs, though I lived much more frugally than I do today, but that was not much different than how I lived in China. Like those Chinese immigrants, I came here in search of better opportunities for my family and myself. But I came through much easier means than they. And the advanced education I had in this country has indeed opened better opportunities for me as a professional and for my son's future. Now our life is quite a luxury by Chinese standards.

I came from the same land as the people who had to be smuggled to this country. I had a better life than theirs in China and continue to have a better one than theirs in this country. They didn't have a chance to go to college in China, and they still can't afford to further their education in this country. They had to do dirty, dangerous, and hard physical labor in China, and they continue to work like horses in this country. But they have a trust in this country. They believe that as long as they work hard, they will have a better life, and their children will receive a better education and have a better future. This land does give them more opportunity to make money, and to make a change in their lives, bringing more opportunity for their families. They are willing to work and live like this with the hope that their children won't have to work and live like they have to, and that their children won't have to take the jobs nobody wants. We all came for the American dream. With the education I received in both countries, I was able to reach my dream after less than ten years of studying and working in this country. But they have to be the stepping-stones for their children's American dream.

When Their Families Are United in This Country . . .

It is a dream for the people smuggled into this country to finally have their families with them again. It is a long and hard process. They expect life to be much easier for them when their families arrive. They will no longer have to share rooms or beds with others but will have a room or even a whole apartment by themselves.

But it is a shock to most of the women and children when they join their men and fathers in their homes in America. They have traveled from a village with green hills, lakes of lotus, and vast fields with various grains and vegetables to New York's Chinatown, with narrow, dirty streets packed with vendor stands and trash containers overflowing with garbage. Because of financial restraint, often they have to share a small apartment with one or two families, and each family has only a room. It is common among these families that the parents sleep on the bottom bunk bed and the children sleep on the top one. Some families turn the closets into rooms for the children. When the relatives come, human bodies fill every corner, as a student wrote:

> Some people sleep over our house
> We don't have many beds so
> Some people sleep on the floor
> The apartment looks messy
> With mattresses, blankets, bodies
> It's not easy to walk around
> One time, late at night
> I had to go to bathroom
> I tried to walk around the bodies all over the floor
> But I stepped on my uncle's hand
> He woke up, but he wasn't angry
> He said, "Next time, be careful."

The women and children are not prepared for the life they have to live in America before they come; rather, they envision a much better life and a more beautiful place than they had at home. They see places and cities in American movies, TV shows, and photos. It indeed seems like heaven. But when they come to New York's Chinatown, they are so dismayed:

> Chinatown smells.
> Chinatown looks like a garbage town.
> Mice playing around at night,
> Cockroaches looking for their love.
> I don't want to live in Chinatown.

Not only do children feel the pain, but their mothers do as well. Before they even have a chance to feel their new homes in America, they start working. Their husbands can't support the whole family by themselves, and they need their wives' income to make ends meet because they have more people to feed and a bigger place to rent. Besides, they have bigger dreams for themselves and their children. The women don't mind working hard, but they feel as though they have lost their homes and a family life, and they rarely spend any time with their children. This is the hardest thing for these women. A woman from a village in the Fuzhou area expressed it this way:

> My husband smuggled to this country. Eight years later, I joined him with my two children. I was happy as I thought finally we were together as a family. My children were very young when he left China. But soon after I came, I had to join him working in a Chinese restaurant. We worked day and night, and had no time for our children. My husband always wanted to have a restaurant himself. So we borrowed money and bought a small take-out restaurant business in Brooklyn. We always get home after midnight. The children are already asleep when we get home every night, and when they leave for school in the morning, we are sleeping. We have to work seven days a week year-round, and only take Thanksgiving Day off. One day break in a year, that is the only break. My children have to help us after their school and during the weekend, that is the time when our family is together. When the restaurant is busy, the children have to work. When the business is light, they do their homework. I do laundry in the morning before I go to work or after midnight. We don't do anything as a family, but work all the time. I feel so bad for my children, but what can I do? I don't like this kind of life [crying . . .], and don't know when I can live the way I want. I miss China, the way we lived there, and the family I had there. Now, I don't have time for my children; never even have a chance to cook a meal just for the family. . . . [Crying hard, and can't talk anymore].

Many women get depressed, have mental breakdowns, and become very sick. Some commit suicide and some have to return to China. Some have babies, but they have to send them back to China, as they have no time to take care of the babies. Their children notice and feel their mothers' pain. In writing, we hear one student express this:

> My mother is sad,
> She feels sad,
> She looks sad,
> She even sounds sad.
> I want to make her
> Happy again.

Another student wrote:

> My father worked in the kitchen of my uncle's restaurant, and only came home once a week. My mother, brother and I stayed with my aunt. My mother stayed home by herself for a long time, as she couldn't speak Cantonese or English so she couldn't get any jobs even in Chinatown. She was so depressed, lonely and sad while my brother and I were in school. She cried a lot until my aunt got her a job in her garment factory. My biggest wish is my brother and I would learn English fast, so we can help my father and mother.

An eighth grader wrote about her new baby sister. First she started with how excited she was when she heard news of her mother giving birth to a baby sister and she gave her a name, Karen. Then she ended her narrative like this:

> A few days later, my greatest Mom and my pretty little sister both came back from the hospital, and from that moment, our house always had a baby crying, baby laughing, baby screaming and many people came to look at my little sister. Every time when Karen making the moment, all of us were started laughing, because we think she's cute and everything she did was very funny . . . .
>
> Now she's in China. It's my parents, they are too busy. We don't have extra time and people to take care of her. The only thing we can do is to send her back to China. My grandparents were there and they would take care of her.
>
> Now when I go home, I feel the house is too quiet. I miss Karen laughing in my bed and play with me. How come there's nothing now? When I start to think about my baby sister, I would cry, because she brings a lot of fun when she's here. I miss her a lot—Karen!

It is quite common for families to send their babies back to China, and the separation can last until the child reaches school age.

Many people may be puzzled by now and question why, if they had a comfortable life in China, would they come here in the first place? Why did they come to suffer so much for a life they don't like? I asked the same question to both men and women. Their responses were different. The men's responses usually were similar to this:

> It is easy to make money in America. As long as you are willing to work, there are always jobs available. If you work harder, you can eventually have your own business. Our children definitely have better education and future here. They can have free public education and have a chance to go to college in this country. In China, all this is impossible. We are farmers; our children and grandchildren would only be farmers. There everything depends upon who you know, and we are just farmers or labor workers and will stay at the bottom of the society generations after generations. Here we have a chance.

The women were not as positive as their men. A woman from Guangzhou said:

> I didn't know, didn't know why we had to come. Just because everybody says coming to America is a good idea, and so we grew up thinking that was the place we would eventually end up with. My husband was here, and we expected to join him someday. When I first came, I wanted to go back every day and my son too. He said, "Mom, let's go back." I fought a lot with my husband when I first came, as I hated to be there. I was not used to do the work like this [garment factory work]. In China, we had a much easier life. But I am used to it now. What can I do otherwise? I have to get used to it if it is good for my son.

It is the vision of a better life in the future that keeps them here, motivates them to work hard, and helps them tolerate any pain they have to go through. The worst thing for the family is unemployment. Work secures their present life, gives them hope for the future, and makes everything they dream possible. A loss of jobs is a nightmare. The students described what happened when their parents could not find jobs or when they lost a job. One student told about his "hardest time":

> The hardest time was when my father lost his job. Every day he stayed in bed, yelling and cursing. He got mad at me for no reasons, but I didn't cry or even blame him, as I knew he was under stress and in a bad mood. He didn't know how to get unemployment stipend, as he didn't know English. Finally with help of some friends, he got his unemployment stipend. That day he told my brother and me: "You'd better study English hard. If you don't know English, you can't survive in this country. You see, your father is too old to go to school. Even if I could go to school, who would make a living for the family? I put all my hope on you both." After he said this, he went to the bed again and kept silent for days.

In Chinatown, if one doesn't know English or Cantonese (a dialect of Guangdong province) or has no connections, he will have a hard time finding jobs. Most of the old-timers speak Cantonese; they own most of the Chinatown businesses. Social connection is always the key to finding jobs. The people from the Fuzhou area are newcomers and don't speak the dialect. Worst of all, many of them don't have legal papers. So it is hard for them to find jobs, and if they find one, they will be the most exploited. But it is better than nothing. They have to work all the time when they have jobs, as a woman said:

> My husband has been in this country for over ten years, and never gone to any place, but works all the time. We just have to work hard when we have a job. If someday we don't have a job, then we won't regret that we didn't work hard when we had one. You never know what would happen to you someday. In America, we have to depend on ourselves to make a living. In China, we had a large family so we would help out each other if someone were in trouble. Here everyone is struggling to make a living.

The uncertainty and the desire to make quick money and get out of the unbearable working and living conditions, and also to search for some excitement in life, drive a lot of men to gamble. Gambling most of the time worsens their already hard-to-swallow life. The yelling, the fighting, the sadness and frustration make the air heavier at home for the children.

> Pa! A strong and hard hand hit my face
> It was my father, who liked me so much
> Who spoiled me so much.
> But this time, he hit me.
> I felt sad, I felt terrible.
> I hated him, I hated him.
> Because he hit me.
> I ran away, I cried,
> I screamed, and I yelled.
> Pa Pa, did you know?
> You hurt me.
> You hurt my feelings.
> You broke your good, kind
> Image in my heart.

An eighth grader wrote:

> My father
> Likes to gamble
> Sometimes, he does not work,
> He goes to gamble.
> When he comes home late,
> My mother yells at him.
> She says,

"Why do you come home late?
Where do you go?"
When my mother
Yells at my father,
I feel
Like it is raining.
He yells
Like a thunderstorm.
One time,
My father came home late, and when
My mother finished yelling,
They were
Not talking.
That night,
They did not sleep together.
If my father
Does not work,
I can find him in one place,
Every time,
The place
Is in the back of the barber shop [underground gambling place].

Many families have to move out of Chinatown with no notice, as their men must escape from a gambling debt. But life is harder for them out of Chinatown. Many have to move back and start all over again.

In the past three years, I have stayed in Chinatown during my monthly visits to New York. I have become friends with some residents of Chinatown. From them, I have heard many stories of the new settlers in Chinatown and gained an insider's view of the new Chinese immigrants with whom I rarely associate in this country. Being together with them reminds me of my time on the farm and in the factory where I was sent to work during the Cultural Revolution in China. They look at me differently because of my education and my professional work. They admire that I can do well in this world; they seek advice from me about their children's education and feel honored to have me as a friend. But they also laugh at me when I show them my great bargain when, as a matter of fact, I was cheated at a vendor's stand. They teach me how to pretend to be an insider in Chinatown in order to get a good deal and to recognize real-brand products when I make purchases. They share with me their pains, frustrations, and secrets. They cook me the delicate food they know I am not able to get outside of Chinatown. My relationship with them makes Chinatown more intimate for me, and each visit is like a hometown visit, more than just for groceries and real Chinese meals but also to reconnect with my roots and regain my image of being a Chinese.

Though I feel comfortable enough staying in their apartment for my visits, coming back from each visit makes me appreciate more my small-town suburban house and life. I wonder if I have indeed become an American. I remember how miserable I felt when I first came to settle in a life like this. Coming from crowded city life in China, I felt the country life was too lonely for me. The huge space scared me, and seeing pedestrians on the street would excite me. Now I enjoy this American middle-class life, quiet and distant from the crowd and noise, though once in a while I miss the exciting city life and a close relationship with intrusive neighbors.

Recognizing the difference between my present life and my friends' life in Chinatown makes me realize the divisive class distinctions in this country among our Chinese immigrants. Wong (1982) discussed the differences that exist among the Chinese immigrants in social, economic, and educational backgrounds:

> They [professionals] lived mostly in the suburbs and cities among middle-class White Americans. Many of these intellectuals looked at Chinatown with disdain. They felt that Chinatowns are not representative of China and considered the residents of Chinatown to be "low class" and "barbaric," since they were not highly educated. (63)

I remember a conversation about the residents in Chinatown I had with a Chinese friend who shares my background:

> I don't like to be identified with those people. They were farmers back in China, uneducated and uncivilized. I hope the American people don't think we Chinese all are like them. We even don't look like them. With the residents like that, that is why Chinatown is so dirty, so backwards. They have no manners: spit, litter, and pour dirty water on sidewalks. They give us Chinese a bad image. I am embarrassed to be associated with the people like that.

The new settlers in Chinatown came mainly from the working class in China and continue this status in this new world. They were looked down upon in their homeland and continue to be discriminated against and exploited by their own people in this land. In Kinkead's words, they are "Chinatown's 'invisible' people, the new immigrants working in its garment shops and restaurants, who speak no English" (1992, 6). They are trapped in the lowest of the low status after they have sacrificed so much to move far away from their homeland and started a new life all over again in a new world. They came to America, but they don't know how Americans live outside of Chinatown except from what they see on TV, and they and their children have little contact with American people except schoolteachers. They don't even know much about New York City outside of Chinatown. But they have a hope that the education their children receive in this country will change the status they were born into and help their children have a better life and future, as one mother said to me:

> I want our son to have a better education. We will let him go as far as he can, and do whatever he can. But if he can't go far in education, then at least he knows English well. He can help us run our own garment shop. My husband always dreams to have his own garment shop, but it is impossible to have your business without knowing any English.

We all push our children to study hard, but the difference between the people in Chinatown and people like me is that they don't have time and don't know how to help their children with their schoolwork and don't know how to help them advance their education in this country. They depend entirely on the school and the children themselves for their children's education.

Content Knowledge and Bilingual Education— Preparing Students for Learning and Living in America

In addition to the language and cultural barriers, most of our new Chinese immigrant students are not prepared academically for their education in American schools. They are generally at least a year behind the grade they are assigned to when they come to American schools. In China, the children in the cities start their first grade at age six, just as children do in this country, but in the villages, which are economically underdeveloped, children begin formal schooling at the age of seven. Usually they have not attended any day care, kindergarten, or preschool before their first grade. Also, China's compulsory education (grades 1–9) applies only to big cities, not to villages or small towns. According to statistics in the late '80s, an official in Beijing stated, "about 2.7 million children, 6–12 years old, were unable to go to school at the time" because there was a shortage of schools and teachers (Xie 2001). Many families in villages don't even send their children to school at the age of seven. When those village children come to America, they are assigned a grade level according to their age but not according to the previous grade they attended in China. Among our newly arrived immigrant children, many had only three or four years of formal schooling in China before they attended sixth or seventh grade in our school.

The poor preparation for American education among our new Chinese immigrant students is in accordance with recent studies about education in China. A report in the *New York Times* (Sachs 2001) stated that only 9.8 percent of the thirty-three million people in the Fuzhou area complete high school. An American educator who recently visited China reported, "The illiteracy problem is compounded by school dropouts. An official in Beijing mentioned that about 10,000,000 children leave school each year" (Howard 2001, 4). Most of the new Chinese immigrants in New York's Chinatown came from villages in the Fuzhou area and belong to this reported group. Worst of all, most of our newly arrived Chinese didn't grow up with parents around and were brought up by their grandparents, who had never gone to school. Among them, many grew up with no books around in the house and received little help with schoolwork. Also, since they were little, they were told that some-day they would join their parents in America. They and their families didn't see the point of going to school in China; rather, they thought it would be wasteful to study in Chinese since they would have to relearn everything in English when they arrived in America. Therefore, many of them never paid much attention to learning during their primary school years. Many never picked up a book or read anything outside of school in China.

I also found out in my interviews that because of China's one-child-per-family policy, families with two children are required to pay more for the education of their second child. So many of these families chose not to send one of their children to school. That is often the case for girls. Among our new students, there are always a few girls who had barely any formal schooling and can hardly write their names. When these children come to our school, they are put in sixth grade or higher because of their age, not because of their previous schooling.

With this kind of (or lack of) previous educational background, the recent Chinese immigrant students encounter tremendous difficulties in our school, especially in the subject areas. The ESL program in IS 131 used to be inte-grated with social study content. It had been a huge challenge for ESL fac-ulty to teach both a new language and at the same time a full middle school social studies curriculum to these new immigrant students. With limited English skills and vocabulary, the students couldn't go far in their learning of content knowledge. And the ESL teachers were always frantically looking for reading materials with social studies topics written in simple English. The simplified texts, though their language might have been at the level of the learners, could hardly meet the requirements of the middle school curriculum or satisfy the interest of the middle school–aged learners.

This awkward situation had been frustrating the ESL as well as subject area faculty for years. The English teachers complained about the students' lack of basic knowledge of literature, and the science teachers didn't know how to explain science concepts to them when they didn't even understand the concepts or vocabulary in their native tongue. The social studies faculty complained that they didn't know how to begin to cover the curriculum required for each grade, which was Egyptian civilization for sixth grade, twentieth-century American history for seventh grade, and world history for eighth. I could feel the faculty's frustration, especially after seeing how hard a science teacher tried to teach a lesson about cloud formation. She tried every strategy she could think of to engage her students, but few of them could understand what she was saying. From my own ESL learning experience, I could sympathize with the students: when the students are bombarded with a new language and new knowledge, they must be totally lost. As an educator, I could also understand the teachers' frustration. Facing this huge challenge, I was just as frustrated as the faculty and as lost as the students. At that point, I doubted myself if I could ever be any help to the school.

At a faculty meeting, a social studies teacher reported: "These children have no knowledge of American history. They thought Columbus discovered America two thousand years ago and that the American Civil War took place in 1945. When asked where New York City was, they pointed at where New Mexico was on the map." I was so shocked. It suddenly occurred to me that these children needed not just the content knowledge for their middle school education but also (to me more important) the necessary knowledge to be new Americans. I couldn't imagine myself moving to a new city and having no idea of where it was on the map, or relocating myself to a new country knowing so little of that land. Afterward, I couldn't stop thinking of these youngsters: why don't we teach them something they need for their new lives and about their adopted homeland first, rather than being worried so much about covering the mandated curriculum? They have to know about America first, I thought to myself, which should be their first social studies subject, not those concepts required in the curriculum. Why not let them learn about America in the Chinese language arts class, which all new arrivals have to take?

An "Historic Change" in the Chinese Language Arts Program

The Chinese language arts program existed for years and served one-third of the student population, the majority of whom were newly arrived Chinese immigrant children. When I first visited the Chinese language arts classes, it was like visiting classes in China, where the students studied Chinese language, history, and geography. They also read Chinese classic literature and memorized classic Chinese poems. The students developed their fluency and skills in Chinese reading and writing, and in publishing stories, prose, and poems in the local Chinese newspapers. But it seemed that the Chinese language arts program was very much by itself and the students' studies in CLA had little to do with their other literacy learning at school. Since none of the administrators and few faculty at the school understood written Chinese or could speak Mandarin (standard dialect) Chinese, the faculty of the Chinese language arts program were mostly left alone. In the CLA department, there were three veteran teachers, fluent in both Chinese and English, who received their graduate degrees in the United States. There was little communication or collaboration among these three teachers, and each instructor had his or her own curriculum and agenda. They each decided what and how to teach according to their interpretation of the requirements of the state bilingual program. Alice didn't like the program being isolated by itself and wanted to include the CLA faculty more into the school community and see how they could contribute more to overall literacy learning for the newly arrived students.

Many parents whose children were not doing well in their English study didn't appreciate the children's good performance in their Chinese learning. One day, a parent came to one of the teachers, waving her son's composition written in Chinese, and cried out: "My child came to the school since last September, now it is March, how come he still can't speak a word of English? How come? What happens?" Many parents didn't want to have their children in the CLA program even though they were doing well there.

At first, when I saw what little impact the students' study in the Chinese language arts class had upon their English learning and how few connections there were between what these students learned in CLA and in other subjects, I agreed to some degree with how these parents felt. I thought of having CLA teachers help build some content knowledge base for these new middle schoolers, but the demand from every department was so overwhelming. Science teachers wanted the CLA faculty to help the students build a basic foundation of knowledge in science in their Chinese class. The faculty of the English department hoped that the CLA teachers could teach students the concepts and different types of literature genres, such as legends, folktales, fables, fairy tales, fiction, and nonfiction. With this literary knowledge built in Chinese, the students would learn easily those concepts and content in English. Social studies faculty wished that the CLA program would take over the entire social studies curriculum for the newly arrived students.

With this demand, the CLA department could be easily converted into a tutoring program, or a learning center like a remedial program for other subjects, and CLA faculty would teach everything for other content areas but have no content of their own. Alice and I thought hard on this and didn't think we should dump all the problems on CLA and rely on one department to shoulder them all. Chinese was the primary language for most of our students, and the CLA program was too valuable to become a subordinate program to other subject areas. After hearing about the reports of our students' lack of knowledge of America, I realized that we should think about what our students needed to know for their new lives in this new country.

By the end of my first year of visits, when we planned for the coming year, I proposed to Alice and Jane that CLA be integrated with social studies, which used to be covered in the ESL class. All newly arrived immigrant children would take two periods a day of CLA/social studies, whose content would be American history, geography, and government, regardless of the social studies curriculum requirement for each grade. Alice asked Jane and me to propose the recommendation to the CLA faculty and work with them closely in the transition. But after this proposal was formally approved by Alice and Jane and ready to go to the faculty, I started to have doubts. I was worried that this thinking was too radical, or maybe too conservative. I didn't know where I would stand among the ESL or bilingual researchers. I thought of what Freeman and Freeman stressed in their books *Between Worlds* (1994) and *ESL/EFL Teaching: Principles for Success* (1998): the importance of children developing their first language literacy and knowing their own heritage. Was I proposing something that was against the principles for successful ESL teaching or that might even devalue the students' home language or culture?

Just as I was so uncertain of where I stood theoretically at that time, Maureen presented me with Krashen's book *Under Attack* (1996), which she was reading with the faculty study group. That was like receiving water in the desert. Krashen states "one of the major rationales underlying bilingual education: When we give children subject matter knowledge through the first language, we help them adjust more easily to their new situation, and it makes the instruction they get in English more comprehensible. Because we acquire language by understanding it, this speeds their acquisition of English" (6). Reading Krashen, I thought more about our ESL and bilingual programs.

Our ESL program was integrated with social studies. According to research on bilingual education, this model was poorly designed, because among all the subjects, "language arts and social studies require the most abstract use of language" and "will be the least comprehensible for the new second language learners" (Krashen 1991, 12). Our old ESL program integrated two of the most difficult subjects: English language arts and social studies. In the ESL class, our new immigrant students were learning the social studies content required by each grade, which mostly was written in academic English, while developing basic listening, speaking, reading, and writing abilities and vocabulary, spelling, and grammatical competence in English. The students' poor performance in ESL/social studies was due to their "exposure to incomprehensible input most of the day" (Krashen 1996, 11). And our old Chinese language arts program functioned as a maintenance program for the children's primary language and culture, which had little connection with the students' other learning and provided students with little help for their transition into the new language and culture. In other words, CLA stood more as an isolated content subject rather than playing an integral role across the curriculum or supporting the students' overall learning.

I also thought of my own learning as an EFL/ESL student. When I was studying Shakespeare in China, I had tremendous problems understanding either the language or the content of his plays. I wanted to appreciate this world-known playwright and his great works as an English major. So I read those plays in Chinese translation and watched the plays with Chinese subtitles before I read Shakespeare's original works. Though Shakespeare's language still presented difficulties to me, I was less frustrated, as I knew the whole stories and the relationships between the characters in those plays. When I was in class, I could focus my attention on the professor when he explained the puns, the idioms Shakespeare used, and also the differences between modern and Shakespearean English. At that time, without any knowledge of bilingualism, I thought I was cheating, or taking a shortcut in my learning.

After reading Krashen and reflecting upon my own learning experience, I concluded that Chinese immigrant children in Chinatown were a particular type of ESL student. They were surrounded by their primary language and home culture inside and outside of the school every day. Most of them lacked the subject matter knowledge for middle school learning and came from low socioeconomic backgrounds. They needed an effective education that would help further their schooling and, in addition, help their transition into the new language and the new culture. Among many models, Krashen (1999) discussed the "gradual-exit" one, which matched what I proposed. It recommends that subject matter be "taught in the primary language only until the child knows enough English to follow instruction in English. 'Transition' occurs gradually, a few subjects at a time, as they become comprehensible" (77). Cummins (1986) and Krashen (1996) both recommend using the native language to build content knowledge and cultivate cognitive academic language proficiency, which according to the Cummins study, takes five to seven years to develop. I was so happy to find the theoretical ground for my thinking.

But was it wrong to have CLA teach about America but not about China? The words of Freeman and Freeman (1998) rang loud in my ears as they strongly advocated the development of the students' first language and home literacy. I shared my fear with Alice, and she said: "I don't care about what theory says as long as the teaching benefits the children, their well-being, their education, and their success in learning."

I continued to question myself: if we let new immigrant Chinese students learn about America but not about China in CLA, would it take them away from learning their own cultural heritage and identity? This made me look into our students' living environment in New York once more. Living in Chinatown, our students have enough opportunity to maintain their home culture and language. What they lack is a chance to know the world outside of Chinatown, an opportunity to know others and communicate with English speakers. The education our students receive in the school should help them go beyond what they are immersed in every day and help them connect to and prepare for the larger American life. We need to respect our children's home culture and language, but this respect should help them enter the new culture, further their education, and forge their new identity in this new world rather than simply maintain a unique culture and language.

Teaching and Learning in the New Chinese Language Arts Program

Before Jane and I formally proposed the changes to the CLA faculty, I shared my thoughts with individual CLA teachers while visiting their classrooms and during my debriefings with them. They generally agreed to the idea for three main reasons. First, they wanted to play an important role in the students' overall learning, so both parents and students would see the importance and necessity of their learning in CLA. Second, they wanted to be included more in the school community professionally, to share, to plan, to learn, and to work together with other faculty. Third, integrating social studies into the CLA class meant reducing by 50 percent the number of students they had to teach and doubling the instruction time for the students they would have. In the old program, the students took an hour each day of CLA. For the faculty, the teaching load was five hours a day, which meant they would teach five different classes every day, and at least 150 students (30 students minimum in each class). In the new program, the students would take both CLA and social studies with the same teacher, for at least two hours back-to-back every day (students would be required to take eleven hours a week in CLA/social studies). This integration would benefit the students as well as the teachers.

But they had only the summer to design a brand-new curriculum and prepare themselves to teach a subject they had never before taught and were not trained to teach. At the meeting, Jane expressed full support from the school in terms of providing a book budget, time for preparation, and cross-department assistance. The three teachers all felt good and excited. The trust and attention given by the school administrators made them also feel important and valued.

The first challenge the CLA faculty faced was finding books about American history and geography written in Chinese. There were a few textbooks available, but none were very interesting. One teacher took a trip to

China and found a few books on American historical figures written in the narrative genre. Some worked with the faculty in the social studies department, searching for reading materials. They also spent days in local libraries, bookstores, and on the Internet, where they found much written in English yet little written in Chinese. So they translated picture books on the Civil War and stories of slavery into Chinese. With a limited amount of resources, they began the new program in the fall.

In the new program, the CLA faculty, from the very start, worked as a team to design the curriculum with help from the social studies faculty. They shared books they had found through different channels. They also shared their translated work and expanded their teaching territory by reaching out to ESL faculty for teaching strategies and frequently consulting social studies faculty for help with the content. While teaching new content and trying new approaches, they were educating themselves not only about the social studies subject matter but also about ESL instruction.

The teamwork didn't take autonomy away from our CLA faculty. Even though they all taught the same content, American history and geography, they each approached instruction in their own way, with a self-chosen focus. With a brief survey of American history, the sixth-grade teacher, Jian Zhou, chose three aspects of history as his focus: the Revolutionary War, the Civil War, and the American government. With this focus, three presidents were studied: George Washington, Abraham Lincoln, and Bill Clinton. He selected chapters from the books he purchased from China and used picture books he translated from English into Chinese. He often started his class by simply telling historical stories, which captivated all his students' attention and curiosity. When he paused for questions, many hands were raised, and confidence appeared on the students' faces. In the old program, Jian had his students sit in rows, all facing to the front, like they did in the schools in China. Now he had six groups of desks in which students faced one another. They worked in groups, asking questions, discussing the learned materials, and collaborating on the projects. Jian was amazed that his thirty-six students could work so well in groups, even with new students coming in throughout the year. On the walls both inside and outside of his classroom were his students' works, written in both Chinese and English (see Figures 2–1 through 2–3).

The seventh-grade teacher, Shirley Yang, started her new year with a focus on New York City. She believed that her newly arrived immigrant students should know the city they now called home. First of all, she had her students think about what they would like to know about New York, and then she took them to the local public library. They all obtained library cards and started their own research on New York based on their group-chosen inquiry topics. Through research and group presentations, they learned about the history, the

Figure 2–1 Poster of Study on American Government

Figure 2-2 Poster of Study on Federalism

30

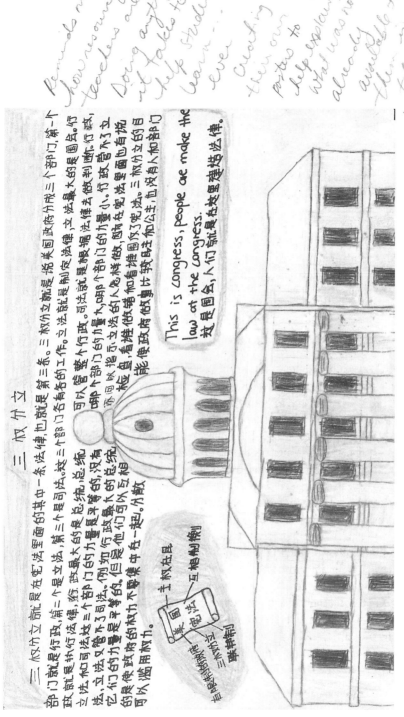

Figure 2-3 Poster of Study on the Constitution

31

population, and the different ethnic groups in New York City, the city's bor-
oughs, the traffic system, and the history of Chinatown in New York. And they
wanted to know more: Why do rich people live in Manhattan and poor people in the Bronx? Why do Chinese people choose Chinatown and Queens to
settle in? Why is Chinatown so dirty? Even when they studied the Civil War
and slavery, the students continued to ask what New York was like during that
time and why New Yorkers were against slavery. Shirley's students loved to
give group presentations and make books. In addition to making their own
books, they each also contributed a page to the big class books about New
York City, the Civil War, and slavery. Among the book collection authored by
the students, there were biographies of George Washington, Abraham Lincoln,
and Harriet Tubman and information books on the Civil War, the American
Pilgrims, the first American settlers, and the history of Chinatown. These books
stayed in the class library and have become reading material for subsequent
students.

Connected Learning in CLA

The social studies content in CLA covers a wide range of American history:
from Native Americans, to Columbus' discovery, to the Revolutionary War, to
the Civil War, to slavery, to immigrants, to Western expansion, to World War II,
to the American government. The students read textbooks, fiction, nonfiction,
and children's books in both English and Chinese. In addition to doing
question-and-answer exercises and memorizing facts, they discuss events, do
inquiry projects, and write compare-and-contrast essays to connect their learning. Among the students' work, I am most impressed with their connected
learning in CLA. When they study one topic, they compare and contrast what
they have learned before and now. For instance, during their study of slavery,
they compared the suffering of the slaves with that of the Native Americans.
Later, when they studied immigration in the 1920s, they not only compared
the new immigrants with the early Pilgrims but also connected all the suppressed people in American history—Native Americans, black slaves, and new
immigrants—in their discussion. Of course, they naturally contrasted the experiences of the early Chinese immigrants and their own experiences. Through
connecting the learning to their personal experience, they realized they were
much more fortunate than the early Chinese immigrants. The following is an
excerpt from a piece written by a sixth grader in English:

> The development of science has made Chinese's journey to the U.S. easier.
> When early Chinese immigrants came, the only transportation was ship be-
> cause at that time airplane was not invented. Then they were on the boat they
> had a difficult time. They did not have fresh foods to eat. They didn't have

enough space to [too] so they had to squeeze to each other. When my parents and me came to America, we came by an airplane. At the airplane we enjoyed fresh foods and plenty of space. We even had different TV programs to watch.

The change of American government's immigration policies greatly affect immigrant'[s] life. When the early Chinese immigrants came to America, the American government treated them as second-class citizens. At that time if a Chinese immigrant was beat up by an American, the government rarely published [punished] the person who did the beating. Now the government treats all immigrants just like Americans. People with different cultural backgrounds respect each other in this great nation.

I was glad to see many students display a positive look at the American nation and their own experiences through this contrast.

The students loved to compare wars, and they were fascinated by the wars that took place in American history, each one of which made the country different. After they studied the Civil War, they compared it with the Revolutionary War and found the similarities and differences in the causes, results, and consequences. Usually the teacher would first have the students do this compare and contrast exercise in groups before they drafted their essays. In their discussion, they talked about the wars and also the leaders, George Washington and Abraham Lincoln. In a group, one student raised an interesting question during the discussion: "If George Washington were the president during the Revolutionary War and started the war, would he have been killed like Abraham Lincoln after the war?" His question was brushed away by his peers, saying. "That was impossible because America was not even a country that time, how could Washington be a president?" Though the boy didn't say more, I was amazed by this boy's question. His question implied if a president starts a war, does he run the risk of being killed? I was impressed by this boy's thinking and the connection he was able to make.

After the discussion in class, the students would work on their comparison essays. Following is an excerpt from a typical comparison essay on this topic:

The cause of the American Revolutionary was that the British government was asking for too much taxes. The colonists couldn't pay it. The cause of the Civil War was because of slavery. In the North there were no slaves because they had lot of factories and stores. They didn't need slaves and they thought that having slaves was no good because slaves were human being also. But the South didn't think that way. There were a lot of plantations in the South, but not much stores and factories. The people in the South needed slaves to work for them. So the North and the South were arguing about slavery. Later the South decided to leave the Union. Then the Civil War Began.

The student ended her essay as follows:

> The results of the two wars were the same because during American Revolutionary War the American won the war. In the Civil War the South leave the Union. At the end of the war the North won the war. So in the both wars Americans had won the war.
>
> In this two wars there were a lot of people died. And a lot of people lost their family members. I think that is very sad. War cause people lose their home and family. I hate wars.

Sometimes a student or two would do their comparison essays differently than the others, and usually their writing turned out to be more interesting. Instead of comparing the Civil War with the Revolutionary War, a student decided to write a different piece as a report of his study of the Civil War that concludes:

> It is not good that brother fight against brothers because it makes a family no safety and peace. No safety and peace can make a family very unhappy and poor. It is a good thing that after the Civil War the American people understand this and they never fight against each other again. This is why the United States is the most powerful country in the world today and so many people want to come to this country.
>
> China is a big country. Chinese people are smart. But China is not a very rich and powerful country in the world. Why? My father told me that there are too many civil wars in Chinese history. Fighting kills people and damages economy. I think this a reason why China is not strong like America. I hope people in China understand this and be friendly to each other. I will write letters to my friends in China. I will tell them brothers in a family should not fight against each other. People in a country should not fight against each other. No fighting a family will be safe and happy. No fighting a country will be strong and powerful. *Powerful to read this on 9-11.*

This piece demonstrated not only his newly learned knowledge about the American Civil War but also his new perspective gained toward China. Through the comparison of the two countries, this student realized what had made America a country which people from all over the world come to join and why China lags so economically as compared with many other countries in the world.

The students were always encouraged to make comparisons between America and China. Since the CLA teachers had knowledge of both countries, they could help and join them in the discussion. During their study of American history at different periods, they compared America's colonial time with China's imperial period; they linked America's slavery system with China's feudal system; they contrasted democratic government with communist society; and they were also puzzled about why World War II books didn't mention Japan's invasion of China, which lasted eight years. Through these comparisons and contrasts between what the students are learning and what they know about China, the students gain not only a good understanding of America but also a different level of understanding of China.

They also like to link America's past to its present. After the teacher gave a brief talk on the wars America fought outside of its land, the students, in groups of six or seven, continued their comparison and contrast of American's role in World War II, the Korean War, the Vietnam War, the Gulf War, and the current war in Afghanistan. I joined a group and was amazed by the discussion (conducted in Chinese). A boy started first:

> Except the current war in Afghanistan, the Americans fought all the other wars to help others. For instance, they joined World War II to help Europeans, fought the Korean War to help the South Koreans, and in the Vietnam War, they helped the south regime in Vietnam, and then helped Kuwait fight against Iraq in the Gulf War. Only in this Afghanistan war, it is for America's own revenge after the September 11 terrorist attack.

Several students agreed with him and one added his words:

> Americans love to help others, that is to keep them to be the superpower in the world. Now, we are suffering, and look what the Arabs did to us in New York.

A girl joined the discussion softly:

> I think the Americans fought all the wars for themselves. In World War II, they joined the war only after the Pearl Harbor attack. They fought the Korean and Vietnam Wars to prevent Communism from gaining power in the world. That is also for their own ideas. Then they fought the Gulf War for the oil supply.

Another girl added:

> In China, we call America the imperialist, because they go to other countries to fight . . .

A boy cut in:

> You can't say that about World War II and the war in Afghanistan now. They are the wars for justice, to fight against German Nazis and to fight the Muslim terrorists.

Another student joined in:

> My great uncle died in the Korean War. My grandpa told me that he was killed by Americans.

A girl said:

> But my great-aunt told me Americans helped us fight against Japanese during World War II. Japanese killed a lot of Chinese in China.

Another girl tried to pull the group back to discuss the Vietnam War:

> How about the Vietnam War—the American people were against this war themselves.

A boy followed:

> But nobody is against our war in Afghanistan. We hate those terrorists and want to kill them all. They kill so many here in our city. And it is hard to find jobs now.

Another student joined his discussion:

> Yeah, the first time, America was invaded like this and suffered by the outsiders' attack on its own land. Of course, we have to fight back.

I was impressed with their knowledge, the connections they made from one war to another, and also their confidence in expressing their opinions. Though they didn't discuss the Vietnam War that much, they certainly knew a lot about wars and why the Americans fought those wars. From their family stories, they also knew in what war China was the enemy to Americans, and in what war Chinese and Americans were friends. It is interesting to notice how they shifted their positions when they talked about different wars. When they talked about the current war in Afghanistan, they felt more personally connected and referred it to as "our war" and identified themselves as Americans by saying "We have to fight back." By living so close to the World Trade Center, they were all deeply affected by the September 11 attack. Before then, it seems that they had never felt so American.

During election time, they voiced their opinions about Republican and Democratic Parties regarding who supported immigrants, social service, and labor unions. They pay great attention to the AIDS epidemic in Africa, terrorist bombings, fighting in the Mideast, and other global current events. Reading, writing, and talking about historical and current events have prepared these students to function as literate citizens in this new world and enabled them to foster their new identities as Chinese Americans. Through the development of this kind of thinking ability and broad interest and knowledge in their first language, our students are preparing in our new CLA program not only for their education in America but also for their present and future lives in this democratic world.

The Result of the Reform in the Chinese Language Arts Program

We started this CLA reform during the second year of my visits. In the past four years, the CLA faculty has worked more collaboratively with the ESL faculty, planning the same units on American slavery, immigrants, and Native Americans. The teachers in the ESL and social studies departments have all expressed that our newly arrived Chinese immigrant children are much better prepared in many ways since they have been in the new CLA program: they have a better knowledge base, they learn English faster, and they are more comfortable with expressing themselves in English. Also, they experience a smoother transition to mainstream classes. The CLA program has become an essential part of our overall school curriculum, and its faculty plays a central role in the students' learning.

Since the CLA became integrated with social studies, we have had fewer students and parents complain about their placement in the bilingual program or their learning in CLA classes. The students feel they need the knowledge they learn in CLA class to prepare for their future education and lives in this new world. Some of the students, who come with pretty good English skills, take CLA only for their first year in America. Those students used to complain the most, as they felt they wasted time learning something that had little to do with the new world or with their current or future learning in other classes. They resented having to take the class just because they were newcomers to the country. Now they constantly come back to their CLA teachers for questions related to ESL and other subject classes taught in English. Parents can see the importance of the class and love to hear their children tell them about America, which is knowledge they also need for citizenship. At my last meeting with the faculty, Jian, one of the CLA teachers, commented on the reform we made in the Chinese language arts program as an "historic change" that had made a significant difference in helping students gain the content knowledge they needed for their American education and for their transition to their new lives in the new country.

More Challenges

Since we implemented the change in the CLA program, we have continued to make the program better. In addition to working with individual teachers year-round, Pam and I sit down with the whole group and ask in what way we should make our program better by the end of each year. First, we are making the whole content study more cohesive from grade to grade; each grade reserves certain historical periods as its focus to avoid overlapping content. Second, the CLA teachers are working more closely with the ESL teachers in planning the theme studies. This way, the students will learn the same topic in both CLA and ESL classes, and both classes will reinforce the learning and have joint assignments and projects. This collaboration benefits the students a great deal and takes much planning time by the faculty at the grade level. Third, the CLA teachers work closely with the staff developers to search for ways to find a balance between helping students with limited Chinese literacy build content knowledge and helping them develop their first language proficiency and literacy. All this improvement requires the faculty to work collaboratively within the department and across the departments and constantly adjust their teaching to meet the students' needs.

The most challenging problem that continues to face the CLA faculty is how to reach the students whose first language literacy is very limited. Like any other class, a CLA class has students with a wide range of levels. The literacy gap between students at the advanced level and students with limited reading and writing skills can be five to seven years. Because of its heavy content requirement, the CLA course leaves little space to help the students who have limited Chinese reading and writing skills. Usually about 15 percent of the students have very limited literacy skills. These students have limited vocabulary, are unable to express themselves in writing, and don't know how to use punctuation. With this limited proficiency in their first language, they usually have the most problems in their English learning as well. When I read the Chinese writing written by these students, I could tell that they were barely at the first-grade level in Chinese, but they are now sixth graders in America. Usually these students come from families that can give them little help and support for their schoolwork. Though the students can understand their CLA teachers, they have a hard time keeping up with the reading and writing. Their work shows minimum progress throughout the year.

In the CLA/social studies program, the students develop their first language literacy through frequent reading and writing in Chinese in the context of learning about America, but teachers usually don't have time to teach the basic skills of the Chinese language or literacy conventions. For a majority of the students, this is fine, but for the group at the low end, this presents a problem. Striking a balance between teaching the content knowledge and helping students develop their basic Chinese language skills, especially for the students with limited Chinese reading and writing skills, remains a big challenge in our CLA/social studies teaching.

Throughout this chapter, I may sound as if there has not been any teacher's resistance to the changes we made in the CLA department. That is certainly false. One of the CLA teachers preferred the textbook to trade books and had her students do more worksheets than writing. For three years, Pam and I worked closely with her. She made some changes in her teaching, such as increasing opportunities for group discussion and letting students write more. But her lectures were mostly textbook-bound. Compared with other classes, her students were much less engaged in their learning.   *Yep!*

We kept pushing her to improve, and finally she broke down. She asked to go back to teaching only Chinese language arts, not integrated with American studies. She stated that Pam and I showed disrespect for the Chinese heritage and that we were denying the importance of the students learning their own Chinese culture and language. She also claimed that she had to prepare her students for the Chinese test that is required by the state. She showed me three sets of the Chinese tests and asked me how she could prepare her students for those tests while having to teach American history. Alice, Pam, and I expressed to her that good teaching should put students' interest and *So true.* benefit first, not the test. Eventually this teacher started including more trade books and having students do more writing rather than worksheets in her teaching. We assume she may need to have her own pace for change. Perhaps Pam and I should be more patient and trustful.

3

Developing Students'
Oral English Language
Ability

When I first visited IS 131, I felt like I was back in China. Seeing so many faces of Chinese children and frequently hearing the Chinese language made me feel incredulous that this was a school in America. During my first visit, Maureen give me a tour through every ESL classroom. The school was huge, with four floors, and each floor had three or four stairways. Between classes, when the students changed rooms, we felt run over by waves of student crowds on the stairs trying to get through to their next classes. The students, just like any other children of their age, were loud and naughty: boys pushing each other, girls trying to squeeze through them, and lots of laughing and teasing. But once they were in class, they became silent; it seemed that their faces and bodies were motionless. It was hard to know if they understood the teachers. Getting a word out of them was like pulling teeth. Even when working on group projects, they whispered to each other in Chinese, trying to figure out what they were asked to do. They showed the most confidence when asked to copy from the board.

When I tried to carry on a conversation with a few girls, they looked to one another, blushing and puzzled, and shook their heads with their eyes cast down, whispering in Chinese "don't know." The boys would bravely ask me, "Can you speak Chinese?" When I responded in Chinese, their heads all turned to me, asking for help with the work. I found that most of the students in the ESL program couldn't express themselves well in English, even though many of them had been in U.S. schools for three to four years. Based on my son's first learning experience in an American school and my own English learning experience in China, I was puzzled by the slow development of the English language skills of these new immigrant students.

My son came to this country as a second grader, and after six months in an American school, he became a quite fluent English speaker. By the end of the first year of his U.S. schooling, his reading and writing ability reached his grade level. I studied English in China. After three years of learning English intensively, I could speak, read, and write in English quite well. I understood that these new immigrant students in Chinatown didn't have as good an English language environment as my son did, but at least they were learning English under much better conditions than did I. They were taught English mostly by English-speaking teachers and could practice English speaking, listening, reading, and writing at school all day long. They also had access to TV programs in English at home. Compared with them, I almost had zero access to English speakers or any authentic English language opportunities. If I could learn English well in a non-English language environment, why couldn't they? I assumed that these students didn't work hard enough and our teachers needed to push them harder. My first suggestions to the teachers after my first visit were (1) provide more speaking opportunities in class (small-group projects and discussion), (2) forbid speaking Chinese in the classrooms, and (3) assign students to watch a news program in English every day. I thought that with this kind of push, we would help the students develop their English language skills. Kiran, a seventh-grade science teacher, and Ourania, a sixth-grade ESL teacher, who both worked with Maureen and me closely during the first year, implemented my suggestions.

Kiran and Ourania had their students work more in small groups and required them to speak English. But most of the students became quieter. Also, when they were called on to speak, they gave only one- or two-word answers. The two teachers were very patient and tried every way possible to provide the students with more speaking opportunities, but it was hard to get the students either to talk in groups or to speak up in class. In the past, the students would communicate about their classwork among themselves in Chinese, and now most of them just kept their mouths shut. Kiran questioned me about not allowing the students to speak Chinese in class: "Why can't we let them discuss the work in Chinese? It is better than not saying anything."

"Maybe some Chinese, but not too much," I revised my suggestion. But "how much is too much?" was a question I was confronted with by some teachers. It was a hard question, and I had to do more thinking. I decided to have another look at the living and learning experiences of the new immigrant students in Chinatown.

Our students in Chinatown don't have a good English language learning environment—they can do just about anything in Chinese. They watch Chinese programs on TV, rent Chinese movies, go to Chinese doctors, shop at Chinese stores, and eat in the Chinese restaurants. Even when they eat in McDonald's and Burger King in Chinatown, they can make orders and read the menus in Chinese. These students seldom leave Chinatown to see other parts of New York City. The town is more like an extension of China than a place in America. To our students, learning English is more like learning a foreign language, which is more for the school than for life's necessities. Our classroom is the only place where our new immigrant students have close contact with the English language and English language speakers. We have to maximize our students' English language learning opportunity and stress the development of their oral language ability. But as they are at a very self-conscious age, they don't want to sound stupid or out of control. They are afraid of being laughed at or drawing attention to themselves. For the Chinese, especially the girls, it is intolerable to make mistakes in public.

As an ESL learner, I could sympathize with those students. Even today, having been a professor for a decade in this country, it is still hard for me to speak out in a formal situation without any preparation or to a crowd of strangers. I always need more time to think through an idea and phrase it in what I feel is an acceptable way. I hate to share my half-baked thoughts—so-called thinking in process. If I sense a situation that doesn't allow me enough time to think through an idea, I just prepare myself not to open my mouth.

After I thought about the English learning situation for our new Chinatown immigrant students, and my own experiences as an ESL learner, I came to a new conclusion: we should give students time to prepare what they are expected to do or talk about in class and help them develop their speaking and listening gradually and systematically. Setting up simple rules was just not enough. Not allowing students to speak Chinese in class only made them feel more handicapped.

Listening and Speaking Homework

Developing speaking and listening skills not only is very time-consuming but also involves a lot of self-correction and repetition. In a class with twenty students, the teacher cannot give each student sufficient time and attention to work on his or her speaking and listening skills. We have to rely on students themselves and their time outside of school. It is like learning to play an instrument; learners have to practice a lot on their own before they come to the instructor.

I suggested that we had to let them prepare for what they were expected to do the next day, no matter if it was to read their work, or to present their ideas, or even to read aloud. Without preparation, most of them would keep silent. This meant we needed to give students listening and speaking homework if we expected them to read or say something in class. Students with different levels of English proficiency would have different kinds of speaking and listening homework, but they all needed to have their own tape recorders.

The parents association made the recorders available at the school at the beginning of a new year at a cost of fourteen dollars each. When the new students came to register with their parents, they each were required to purchase a tape recorder. The very beginning English language learners started with pattern books, books with simple language and repetitive patterns.

The teachers taped themselves reading, and the students were given the tapes and books to take home every day. At home, the students first read the books with a dictionary. After they understood the book's content, they listened to the book on the tape, which was made by their teachers. The teacher read the book in a natural speed the first time and then read each line slowly the second time, leaving the student enough time to follow along. By listening to the book as many times as they wanted to, and reading along until they reached fluency, students practiced listening and speaking on their own. Then, they taped their own reading into the recorder (many times deleting and retaping until they were pleased) and turned in their tape to the teacher the next day. This may sound boring and noncommunicative, but our students don't have access to an English language environment or to anyone that can read to them or communicate with them in English, so they have to learn on their own. Students learned English in China this way, making the best out of nothing.

When this idea was first implemented, the problem facing the teachers was to find time to make the books on tape. They were so overwhelmed by the time they had to spend checking each student's homework on tape. Many teachers preferred to use the commercial books on tape, with music in the background. The first problem with that was those books tend to be above the English level of our beginning learners. They are made more for content listening rather than the language. Second, the books are read too fast for our beginning students to follow along. They could get a feel of the language by listening to the tape but couldn't understand or practice speaking or listening skills with it. Those commercial books on tape are good for more proficient English language learners, but not for the very beginning ones.

John Lo, an ESL teacher, found an efficient way to reduce the time spent on book taping. Before he let his students take books home, he would work with them in small groups (five to six students), going over the books with them and reading to them. While he was reading the book, the six students would place their recorders right in front of him. He would read in a natural way first and then at a slower speed. In this way, he didn't have to spend extra time taping his reading, making copies, and labeling the tapes. Also, he could significantly reduce the management for the tape collection in his class library. One student thought of a better way to improve the recording; he brought a microphone to clip on John's shirt so he could get a better recording. That idea was well adopted by his peers, and soon John looked like he was hooked on multiple leashes.

John also found a manageable way to check on his students' listening and reading homework. "Usually," he told me in the interview,

> I would listen to their tapes in the car on the way home or to school, or some-times while I was reading the students' work. I don't have to listen to their reading from the beginning to the end, but just get a feel if they are serious about doing their work. You know, often, I don't have to even listen to the tapes. By hearing how they read in class, I just know if they have practiced their listening and reading at home. If they do it, they would read and speak much better, and with more confidence participating in class.

The speaking and listening homework for the students with greater proficiency is different from that for the very beginners. They listened to more advanced books on tape (some are commercial ones), they pay more attention to individual words or pronunciations, especially those they have difficulty pronouncing, and they prepare their talks and speeches on the tape. Some very motivated students continue to practice their listening and speaking this way on their own, not just for the teachers or for a homework assignment.

The benefits of assigning speaking and listening homework can be con-cluded as the following:

- It directs students specifically to practice speaking and listening skills on their own.
- It saves class time and has students prepare themselves before the class.
- It frees the teachers to deal with more challenging problems rather than drill-and-practice work.
- It provides a way to help the students who don't have outside access to a good language environment or proficient English speakers.
- It trains students to notice and self-correct their own speaking and pro-nunciation problems.
- It cultivates independent learners.

The speaking and listening homework is closely connected with class oral language activities. The self-regulated speaking and listening homework and teacher-directed oral activities in class are codependent in our language instruction for developing the students' English listening and speaking skills.

Speaking, Listening, and
Oral Language Activities in Class

Before my work in IS 131, I heard about a thirty-year-old Chinese American man who was born and grew up in Chinatown but could barely speak any English. I couldn't believe it. How could this be when he had gone through many years of education in American schools? When I saw how little English the students spoke in and out of class when I first came to work in IS 131, I thought of that Chinese American man. We could easily let our students fall through the cracks like that man if we didn't pay special attention to developing their oral language ability. For our Chinatown new immigrant students, we had to work very hard on developing their speaking and listening skills. In the past four years, we have searched for and experimented with many possible ways and constantly improved them to provide our students with more listening and speaking activities in our instruction.

Listening Center

To provide our students with more listening opportunities in class, I recommended that every classroom have a listening center with a tape recorder with multiple earphone jacks and books on tapes (teacher-made and commercial ones). It didn't take long for Alice and Jane to make this happen in every classroom. But to manage the listening center and to keep five or six students working at the same pace was not as easy as I thought. When we first sent five or six students to the listening center, they didn't know what they should do when they finished listening to a tape. Some students had problems following along, so they were totally lost. Some boys used that time to have fun with each other. We realized that the students needed specific instructions on how to work as a group at the listening center. At the listening center, the group of students (very beginners) would be given a basket with a tape with five to ten pattern books recorded on it and six sets of books, and given the following general directions:

- Listen to the books quietly twice.
- Listen and repeat with the reading three times.
- Turn off the tape recorder to practice reading by yourself or with a peer twice.
- Listen to the tape again twice.

Teachers would vary their directions according to a specific lesson and their knowledge of their own students. To illustrate how the center was used,

I will share one specific lesson on how to write a self-introduction. The teacher wrote a piece about herself and recorded it on the tape for the students to listen to at the listening center. Following are her directions for the group assigned to the listening center:

> After we go over this piece [a piece about the teacher herself] together as a class, you will listen to it on tape. At the listening center:
>
> - Listen to it twice.
> - Stop the tape and read aloud to yourself and underline the words you have difficulty reading.
> - Listen to it on tape again and repeat after it, paying special attention to the words that are hard for you. Do this three times.
> - Turn off the tape recorder and practice reading in pairs.
>
> When it is your turn to come to the teacher, the teacher will
>
> - check your reading
> - have you tell her what you have learned about her from reading this piece
> - have you ask her questions: What do you want to know more about her?

At first, the students had problems understanding these detailed directions. The teacher had to explain them and have students explain them to each other in Chinese. After a few times, the students learned the routine. With specific instructions, especially when tailored to a specific lesson, the students knew what they should do during and after listening to the tape. The specific directions not only teach the students how to monitor their work at the listening center individually but also set rules for managing groupwork. For our very beginners, many teachers rely quite a lot on the listening center for the students to prepare and review new lessons.

Guiding Students in
Their English-Speaking Development

Learning to speak a new language is always hardest for older ESL learners, especially for our new immigrant middle schoolers in Chinatown. Their age, their culture, and their living environment all contribute to their slow development. It is not enough to just provide oral language opportunity, but teachers have to systematically guide the students. I have learned this from observing how our teachers tried different strategies in helping their students develop their language skills and also by working with the teachers to make their teaching more effective. I observed Shirley Yang and John Lo, two ESL teachers who are bilingual speakers, working with their new immigrant students. I interviewed Shirley and John afterward about how they systematically planned their lessons to aid the development of their students' speaking ability.

Shirley is an eighth-grade ESL teacher (who used to be a CLA teacher). One of her classes was made up of eighteen newcomers, many of whom came at the beginning of the school year and some who arrived only one or two months before my visit. None of them could speak any English when they came. Every day, she began her class with a morning message or daily news, which was usually about the date, weather, class attendance, and class news. In doing this every day for ten to fifteen minutes, her students not only practiced and reviewed their speaking skills by describing their day but also learned to speak at least one or two new words or sentences every day. One specific example I recorded was like this:

Shirley writes and reads aloud what she writes on the easel. She leaves space for the students to fill in their words or phrases.

Shirley: Today is . . .

Students: Tuesday, December 11.

Shirley: [*writes down the students' words and reads them aloud*] Do we need a comma or a period here?

Students: Period.

Shirley: The weather is . . .

Students: Cloudy. [*students yell out in Chinese*]

Shirley: [*writes down response and says it in English*] Cloudy. The weather is cloudy. Is it cold?

Students: [*some*] Yes. [*some*] No.

Shirley: Okay, I will write: "It is warm/cold." We have a visitor, one visitor [*emphasizes the singular form*]. Should we put "s" at the end?

Students: No.

Shirley: We have a visitor. Or we can also say she came to visit us. Her or his name?

Students: Her name.

Shirley: Her name is Danling Fu. She is a teacher, too. Which too/two should we use here?

Students: Too, t-o-o.

Shirley: Is anyone absent today?

Students: Meidan and Feng Qing absent today.

Shirley: Meidan and Feng *is* or *are* absent?

Students: Are absent.

Shirley: Anything special about today?

A boy: [*yells out*] Picture day.

Shirley: Oh, yes, it is the photo day. [*she writes this down while saying it*]

A student: [*asks in Chinese*] Why *photo* is not spelled as f-o-t-o? What is the difference between *picture* and *photo*?

Shirley: Picture and *photo* can be the same, but *picture* is used broader than *photo*, which refers to the picture we take but not paint. About the spelling of the word *photo*, that is a good question, but the English language can be very strange. . . .

After Shirley finished this message, she had students read along with her twice and then asked her students to copy it down for homework reading practice. The next day, at the beginning of the class, the students worked in pairs to retell each other this message before they worked on a new message for the day. Shirley's lesson on daily news resembles a lot of "calendar" lessons used for kindergartners. In Shirley's lesson, she stresses the language learning and the oral expressions rather than the concept learning for her beginning ESL middle school learners.

For the first six months of the school year, Shirley used this morning message write- and read-aloud strategy to reinforce the language and skills the students learned (day, week, plural versus singular, verb agreement, punctuation, gender forms, word usage) and teach them some new skills and expressions each day. By spring, the daily news became more complicated and included more about the school, the Chinatown community, or home, or even brief news from the local newspapers. In this way, the students gradually expanded their everyday English vocabulary and expressions and became comfortable talking about their daily lives.

Shirley also used pattern books to systematically develop her new students' speaking skills while teaching them to read and write in English. The following is a whole lesson I had a chance to observe:

On the two columns of the easel board, the teacher writes two questions: *What is on the left side of the classroom? What is on the right side?* The students look around and name what they see on the right side first, then on the left side. They yell out words in either English or Chinese. The teacher writes down the words they give in English. When the students yell out certain words in Chinese, if the teacher knows they know them in English, she insists the students give her those words in English. For example, *flag, map,* and *telephone.*

After the list is completed, the teacher gives a pattern like *When we look to the right, we see . . . When we look to the left, we see. . . .* The teacher leads the class to use the same sentence pattern with the words on the board. Then the students do the same in pairs repeatedly until they gain fluency without reading the words or sentence pattern from the board.

Then the teacher reads the pattern book *Bo Peep's Sheep* to the class. She reads dramatically with her tone and action: *"Little Bo Peep looks right, looks left, looks up, looks down, and looks all around to find her sheep."* After reading it twice, the students can chant together with the teacher without looking at the text. Sometimes, she reads the first page, pauses, and lets the students read the second page on their own. Within one class period, the students learn to say *"look up, look down, look to the right, to the left, and look all around."* After the class reading together, the students get into three small groups: (1) listening center (to listen to *Bo Peep's Sheep* on tape), (2) buddy reading (to practice reading the book in pairs), (3) writing (to create five more new sentences with the same pattern). If time allows, the three groups will rotate their activities.

For homework, the students describe their homes (apartments) in writing with patterns they learned today and practice taping their reading of their writing. The next day, the class starts with students telling about their homes without looking at their writing.

In this lesson, Shirley integrated speaking, listening, reading, and writing. Listening and speaking were the main focus of this lesson. Usually, middle school–aged students don't like to read the pattern books because they think they are too babyish for them. But when they are used mainly for listening and speaking development, the students see them differently. The pattern books are simple enough for them to grab the language patterns quickly and speak them with confidence. By helping the students talk about their own classroom at the beginning of the lesson, Shirley prepared her students linguistically before she read the pattern book to them. She engaged her students, without drilling them, with new sentence patterns and vocabulary. Then she asked the students to use their newly learned language skills to describe their own homes. She didn't restrict her students with one simple book but guided them to apply the skills they learned from the book to their school and home lives. She ignored the may-sound-silly ideas of the book and made the language skills relevant to the students' own lives. With this systematic guidance, the majority of the newcomers in Shirley's class were able to express themselves in class about their daily life experiences with certain confidence within a school year.

John teaches seventh- and eighth-grade newcomers. He said to me, "[his] priority is to help them become able to speak and understand English first. Being able to speak English would help them with their self-esteem and gives them confidence in learning." Before each class began, he stood by his classroom door, and every student had to say to him: "May I come in?" He responded to each one, "Yes, you may." His newcomers all learned to say "excuse me" during the first two months of being in John's class when they would interrupt or move past someone. This impressed me, as it took me five years to form this habit, which is very non-Chinese.

John liked to work with his students in small groups so he could have more close contact with individual students. He spent a lot of time talking about a book's cover, walking through the pictures, and applying newly learned language skills in the context of the students' home and school lives. When working with small groups, he tried to give each student a chance to speak, patiently waiting for their responses. At the beginning, most of the students would respond to him in Chinese. He would give their words back in English and ask them to repeat after him. It was a painstaking process, but John patiently did this with every small group and moved them to gain confidence and skills in speaking. I summarized John's strategies as follows:

- Grab every teachable moment in or between classes.
- Repeat their words (Chinese) and rephrase their responses in English.
- Pay attention to their pronunciations, but don't overdo it to stop them from speaking.
- Allow them to speak Chinese while encouraging them to use English.
- Try to use English all the time.
- Have students repeat their responses in English if you know they are able to.
- Teach students functional oral expressions such as "May I come in?" "Excuse me," and "May I go to the bathroom?" and reinforce their use of those expressions in real contexts.

John also used journal writing to help his students develop their speaking skills. He assigned his students journal writing once or twice a week. They wrote their first drafts at home. John conferred with students during the week to help them revise their writing and help them say what they wanted to express in English. He didn't correct their language word by word or sentence by sentence (that would be too much work) as long as he could understand the meaning. During the weekend the students practiced reading their revised work and talking about their lives into the tape recorder without reading the texts they wrote. On Monday, the students took turns speaking in class, telling the class about their lives. Their journal writing served as preparation for their presentations. At first it was not easy for some students to speak in front of the class. Gradually, with help from the teacher, modeling by their peers, and encouragement from the class, students gained the confidence and ability to present themselves in class.

> We do this once or twice a week and don't have time to do this every day. Sometimes they speak broken English, such as "I in America." I leave them alone, as I believe it is better than never speaking out in English. If they can bravely speak broken English, they will improve their English speaking faster. I pushed everything orally. What is the point of having them write their life experiences, just for me to read? I want them to be able to express, to talk about, and tell others about their lives. I want them to express their meaning first—grammar is not a big deal at the beginning stage—and we will deal with grammar later. Just like letting them write any language in their journals, I let them use any ways to express themselves orally—broken English, English with a few Chinese characters—as long as they tell us about their lives. I want them not to be afraid to speak out, especially in English. At this stage, I help them to write, to speak, to use their writing to speak, to read aloud, to practice using English in public. Our class is their public place, since there is no place in Chinatown they can practice their English speaking. It is hard for them at first, but they struggle, they do it. Now they want to do it.

John eloquently voiced his beliefs. His purpose and efforts in helping the new immigrant students in Chinatown were to develop their English-speaking skills. He worked hard and passionately year-round to push his students to develop their speaking skills. As he said, his students welcomed and appreciated his challenge and help.

On the last day of school, I walked into John's eighth-grade class, with sixteen students who had been in America from a few months to less than a year. The class was learning R. Kelly's song "I Believe I Can Fly." The students read this song the night before, and each translated it into Chinese. In class, they listened to the song on tape together and meanwhile filled in the words in the blanks on the worksheet John prepared. Then they sang along with the tape again and again, louder and louder. The teacher sang together with them, and sometimes he paused the tape to explain the phrases to the class. I could see and feel the passion, the emotion, and the joy flow through the students' voices and moving bodies. This was the last day of the class in their middle school, and this was their first year of their American life. They showed their confidence through their passionate voices:

> If I can see it, then I can do it
> If I just believe it, there's nothing to it
> I believe I can fly
> I believe I can touch the sky
> I think about it every night and day
> Spread my wings and fly away
> I believe I can soar
> I see me running through that open door
> I believe I can fly
> I believe I can fly
> (Oh) I believe I can fly.

The class decided that they would sing this song at their graduation ceremony, as singing this song made them feel as if they could soar in this new land.

In the past four years, I have seen many wonderful presentations and plays given by our ESL students, but I could never forget the first puppet show given by Ourania's sixth graders. She was the first teacher who worked with Maureen and me in searching for effective strategies to develop the students' speaking skills. She worked very hard on this, and the puppet show her sixth graders performed to the whole school faculty in the spring celebrated the first success of her hard work and her students' achievement. This puppet show project started with a lesson on a Chinese folktale: *Er-Lung and the Suns*. After reading it to the class, Ourania was told by many students that the story in English was different from the Chinese version they had read in China. They explained to her the differences and expressed that they wanted to write their own version. Ourania encouraged them and suggested that she would help them write a skit and they would act out. The students were excited about the idea, but few were willing to participate in the show. "So let's do a puppet show," a few students suggested, so they could hide themselves behind the curtain and didn't have to face the audience. Everyone liked this suggestion. Each group was assigned certain parts to write. They collaboratively worked on their parts, line by line, and Ourania had conferences with each group, helping them revise their writing and practice their reading. The class worked hard on this project for months. They created their puppets, designed their own stage, memorized each line, and practiced their ennunciation and expression. They practiced and performed many times at their grade level before they presented their show at a faculty meeting. Many faculty members cried. Alice could not stop her tears. A veteran teacher exclaimed, "My god, this is the best thing I have ever seen in my twenty years teaching at this school!"

[handwritten margin note: I think everyone goes through this feeling when learning or doing something new — at least I can totally relate.]

This was our first show given by our new immigrant students. Many wonderful presentations and shows have followed since then in every grade in the past four years. With experience and improvement, the teachers made the work more manageable, less time-consuming, and more integrated across subject areas. Our teachers and students proved that through our effort and systematical planning and guidance, our shy ESL new immigrant students could succeed in developing their speaking and listening skills despite living and learning in a nonideal English language environment.

Dual Language Instruction in the CLA/Social Studies Program

According to the research on ESL learning (Cummins 1986; Krashen 1999), it takes five to seven years for ESL learners to develop their academic English. We don't have this much time for our students. How can we help our students develop their academic English skills as much as possible when they are with us? Our new immigrant students need to learn English to cope not only with their daily lives but also with their school learning. They need to be able to join book talks and present their knowledge and thoughts at school now and every day. To face this challenge, I presented a brave recommendation to the faculty in the Chinese language arts department: Don't restrict your instruction in Chinese; use English whenever it is appropriate. If possible, please use dual language instruction to maximize our students' English language learning opportunity. In their instruction of social studies content, the CLA teachers would introduce to the students academic language and subject-related terminology. Not only did I realize that my idea presented a great challenge to the CLA faculty, but also I understood that many ESL researchers did not recommend dual language instruction.

I made the recommendation of having dual language instruction in the CLA program based on my own English learning experience and my observation of the instruction in CLA classes. Because of the Cultural Revolution, my formal education was abruptly interrupted. When I went to college in China, majoring in English, I had to start with basic language skills. Within three years, the instructors had to cover the works of Chaucer, Shakespeare, Melville, Hemingway, and Mark Twain while developing our knowledge of basic English language skills such as tenses, variety of sentence structures, as well as listening and speaking skills. It was a tremendous challenge for both teachers and the students. Many of my peers couldn't make it through the literature part of our education because of the lack of academic language and knowledge of classic literature. I struggled very hard and met the expectations. When I recalled how I managed to meet such a demanding requirement,

I realized that I heavily depended on bilingual readings. I read those classic literatures in both Chinese (translation) and English repeatedly and made connections between the two languages. In this way I expanded my knowledge of academic English more effectively than the students who relied solely on English reading. Though my way of learning may not work for others, I believe it should be easier for any learners to use their primary language to learn the complicated ideas behind the academic English, and then have plenty of contact with the terminology (listening to it, using it in speaking and writing) after they have learned about its meaning.

One observation in CLA class made me think: why should we have to use only Chinese in our CLA instruction? One day when I walked into a CLA classroom, I saw the fifty states of the United States were written in Chinese characters on the blackboard. The names of the states were translated phonetically from English into Chinese. I thought to myself: Why not just let the students learn those states directly in English? Why does everything have to be done in Chinese in CLA class, especially when the students study about America? Some terminology must be hard to translate, such as *Underground Railroad, Confederate government*, and *Union government*. That was the first time that I had the idea of having dual language instruction in CLA. I realized it would be challenging for our CLA teachers, but we had to think of our students' benefit first. Since there was so little English language opportunity in our students' lives, we just had to use every possible way to provide our students with more English learning—including the work in our CLA class.

When I talked to the CLA faculty, I met no objections. As a matter of fact, they loved having the opportunity to use English and improve their own English skills themselves, as they didn't have much chance of using English in their lives either. Of course, each teacher used dual language instruction differently in his or her instruction. It purely depended on their different teaching styles and their comfort levels with the English language. They had real autonomy in this respect. I summarized their practices in general as the following:

- *Give general directions mostly in English, such as "take out your notebook" and "get into your groups."* The teachers started the school year with more Chinese for this frequently used classroom language. Two or three months later, they used only English for these kinds of directions.

- *Write the directions and questions to specific lessons in both languages.* Some teachers tended to write complete questions or directions parallel in both Chinese and English. Some only inserted English words and phrases alongside the Chinese sentences. Sometimes, a teacher would write a bilingual sentence: a Chinese sentence with English words and phrases inside, especially the names or phrases with special meaning, such as *Yankees, the Whig Party,* and *Gettysburg Address.*

• *Insert English vocabulary whenever appropriate in your speaking and writing.* I first thought this would be the most challenging for our teachers. But as a matter of fact, I found that our CLA teachers did this quite naturally, though the practice varied from person to person. Because they read a lot of information about America in English, they didn't have to search for English words in their teaching but naturally mixed the two languages together. When they gave a full explanation of certain terminology in Chinese, then gave the students the opportunity to constantly hear and see the English words or phrases in their teaching, this provided a good way to build the students' academic English vocabulary. After understanding the meaning and hearing content-related academic English used in a context, our students learned to use it themselves in both their speaking and their writing.

• *Allow students to use any language for their work in class.* Because the teachers frequently used both languages in their teaching, the students picked up the style and comfortably followed the model in their own talk in the classrooms, in which the main body of the language is Chinese with many English terms and special phrases inserted. The students spoke and wrote in this very bilingual way. I realized that this is exactly how I converse with my Chinese friends in America. Immersed in the English language environment every day, we can't be pure monolinguals anymore.

• *Accept students' work written in two languages.* It is interesting to see the gradual development in the students' writing when they are allowed to use any language in their work. At the beginning of the year, the newly arrived immigrant students wrote their work mostly in Chinese. Then their work was scattered with English words and phrases here and there. Later, some students chose to write certain homework assignments in English. This is very similar to how the students developed their English-speaking ability: from Chinese mixed with English, to broken English, to more conventional English. The teachers focused more on the content and ideas of their writing and only corrected their English language when it affected meaning.

• *Adopt English reading materials in teaching and provide the students with more English learning opportunities.* The main teaching materials utilized in CLA class were in Chinese, but it is hard to find many intriguing books about America in Chinese. There are so many children's books on any topic about America in English. Adopting English reading materials opened up a wide channel for the students' learning. Of course, most of the students were unable to read those English books at first. Gradually, with their learning in both ESL and CLA classes, they began to read more and more children's books in English on the topics they were studying, especially when they studied the same topic in their ESL class. For homework or research projects, our students could choose to read books in either English or Chinese. Many students pushed themselves hard to read the English books.

- *Compare and contrast two language systems.* Though language instruction was not a main focus in the new CLA program, it was hard to avoid talking about the two language systems, since the students used both languages constantly. Sometimes students would initiate questions about the differences in Chinese and English in CLA, as they were not able to ask them in English, such as "Why English has to have tenses? Why we don't have those in our Chinese?" and "Why they use plural forms?" When the students noticed and understood the differences between their primary and target languages, it was easier for them to learn the new rules. Our CLA teachers had knowledge of both languages, and they were able to explain the two language systems and highlight the differences. Through comparison and contrast of the two language systems, our students gained a clear understanding of the English language structure. Though teaching about the structure of language was not the focus of the CLA teaching, the teachers caught teachable moments on this matter, and the students always showed a great interest and had many questions to ask.

With dual language instruction, the CLA faculty contributed a great deal to the development of the new immigrant students' academic English language skills. The students learned and used the academic vocabulary in the context of learning to read, write, and talk about America. As Jian said, "I felt I am also an ESL teacher since I teach so much English in my class. I do love it." Every teacher, no matter if he or she teaches science, math, social studies, or art in IS 131, is an ESL teacher, as almost all of his or her students are ESL learners. We tend to think only ESL teachers teach language, and the others teach subject content. How could that be true when their English language ability affects every subject our students are learning?

With systematic guidance in the development of our new immigrant students' oral English language ability in both the ESL and CLA programs, our new students are not silent anymore. You can hear students reading aloud, presenting their work to the class, performing in class plays, joining in-group discussions, and reading along in the listening centers. The students are sometimes loud, just like when they are in the hallways. They speak English a lot now and love to speak to the teachers. One day during the break between classes, three female seventh graders came to Jian while he was chatting with me and asked him in English: "Mr. Zhou, would you tell us how the power is divided in the American government, the checks and balance system?"

Jian responded to them also in English: "Do you remember what you learned last year about this?"

They replied, "Yes, three parts, the executive, the legislative, and the judicial. They check each other, divide their power, and balance each other. We just want to make sure, because we are talking about this in our social studies class now. Is the president the commander in chief of the U.S. Army?"

Jian responded with a big smile, "Yes, you are right. . . ."

Three years ago, we rarely heard any English spoken by any Chinese students, even in their English class, let alone after the class and to their Chinese language arts teacher—it would have been a miracle.

With their confidence in their language ability as learners, our students are not as shy as they were before. Boys often toss some humor and jokes to show off their English in front of a crowd. We see more smiles on the children's faces and hear more laughter among the children and teachers. The school is not silent and motionless anymore, but full of life and energy and rich with literacy.

Teaching Students with a Wide Range of English Language Abilities

4 奋发图强 努力学习

Each week year-round, new students enrolled in our school, even during the last month of the school year. Most came to the school shortly after getting off the airplane to America. They had no control over when they would come. Once they were granted visas, they had to take off. Their arrival presented a huge challenge to our ESL teaching, as usually those students had to start from learning their ABCs. "How should we help the new arrivals catch up and not interrupt the normal flow of the teaching?" Alice, Jane, and Pam let each grade level group their students according to English language abilities: advanced, intermediate, and beginners. But regardless of how the students were grouped, a gap always existed among the students because of their different learning, reading, and language abilities. It was especially challenging in the beginners classes, where new students came in year-round.

Conducting whole-class lessons or using a core book for whole-class reading can present problems in teaching students with wide ranges of language abilities. This practice has certain limitations for reaching brand-new immigrant students. Like children newly adopted to a family, they need more attention from the teacher. For a teacher, the need to move the class along and meanwhile take care of newcomers can be a big challenge in teaching.

To meet this need, some teachers may keep their whole class at the basic level for quite a while, which can be damaging. I will never forget a lesson I observed during my first visit to IS 131. That was a lesson in a seventh-grade ESL class. A class of twenty-five students were seated in rows. For the first half-hour, the teacher had her students practice writing the letter *A*. While the students were tracing the letter *A* on the worksheets, she circulated from seat to seat, checking everyone's work and helping students with the stroke and

This exists in all general ed. classes too!

shape. I sat next to a boy in the back row and watched him write *A* at least fifty times, ten times the number he was required to do. Then he started to draw while waiting for the teacher to come to his seat. I whispered to him: "Do you like this work?" He shook his head hard with a deep frown on his face. When the teacher finally came to him, she found that he hadn't done the tracing in the exact order as directed and had also done more than she required. She asked him to erase all he had done and rewrite the *A* five times. Only five times, no more. The work took him only ten seconds after she left him. After the teacher finished checking all the students, she went to the front. I thought to myself, "Finally. Let's see what is next." There were twenty minutes left for the class. Surprisingly, she calmly took out another set of worksheets and said slowly and clearly to the class: "Let's practice writing the letter *B*."

When I walked out of that class, my heart cried for the children and their parents. I wondered if it was worth it for them to go through so much pain and continue to suffer all the loss they had endured for the education their children were receiving. But what should we do when some of our students who do need to work on their ABCs are sitting among the students who can read paragraphs? We cannot simply water down the curriculum to slow down the whole class, which would hurt more students in the class.

One day an anonymous note written in Chinese arrived on the principal's desk. It read:

Dear Teacher and the Principal:

How are you doing? I am a student's parent. The reason I am writing to you is that my daughter told me that in her English class, her English teacher asked them to write the exact same thing in their journal every day such as "in the morning, in the afternoon, and in the evening," and gave them the same home-work every day. They work on a book for a long time. And even they practice the same speaking every day. Many students don't want to stay in that class, but they dare not to ask their parents to write to the teacher. They are afraid to be taken to the court if the teacher finds out. Some want the teacher to give them good grades. But my daughter wants to learn, and I am glad that she told other teachers that every parent wants his/her own children to do well at school. If my daughter remains in that English class, I am afraid that she can't learn much. Then that is a waste of time for her to come to school every day. I hope the school can help my daughter switch her class or do something for her. Please don't tell that teacher that my daughter asked me to write this letter to you.

Thanks!

Alice never found out who had written this note, who the student was, or who the teacher was, so she was unable to respond to or act upon this parent's request. But this note revealed that we needed to do more for our students.

Teaching Multiple Groups and Making the Teaching Cohesive

AKA Differentiated Instruction

In order to challenge all students and reach as many students as possible in a class of different language abilities, I recommended teaching in small groups and using multiple books. I believe that teaching in small groups enables a teacher to have closer contact with individual students and adjust her teaching accordingly. When we try to keep the whole class at the same pace, sometimes we may only reach the average; we bore the ones who are above average or higher and confuse the ones who are below average. In order to help all students learn, teaching in small groups is more effective.

For new teachers, it could be a challenge to work with one group and keep other groups on task. I gave demo lessons and workshops on this issue. In my workshop, I presented to the faculty specific models of how they should divide the class into different small groups and rotate working with one group at a time. The following is one of the models I presented at a faculty workshop.

Prior to a lesson, please prepare the students with homework for your next day's lesson, with directions such as these:

- Choose five to ten pattern books for home reading.
- Read to understand the books with a dictionary.
- Practice reading until you read fluently.
- Record your reading into the tape recorder (try to record two good readings).

During the class:

- Start with the class reading aloud: a picture book, not too difficult, but not at a pattern-book level.
- Divide the class into four groups (four to five students in a group). Give each group activity directions and let the students read the directions for one or two minutes and ask if they need any explanation of the directions. Choose a group leader for each group to explain and manage the activity. Samples of the directions for different group activities are suggested as follows:

Group 1: Listening Center
- Listen to the books quietly twice.
- Listen and repeat with the reading three times.
- Turn off the tape recorder to practice reading by yourself or with a peer twice.
- Listen to the tape again twice.

(More advanced students should listen to songs, poems, and picture books or even chapter books. They don't have to go through the same procedure as above.)

Group 2: Buddy Reading Group

- Read to each other with each student looking at the text.
- Talk about the story to each other with both students looking at the pictures.
- Read to each other by using the same pattern used in the book with new vocabulary (work out a word list before doing this activity).

Group 3: Writing/Independent Reading Group

- Read quietly your self-selected book (help them choose the books at their own reading level).
- Write a reading response after the reading.
  - What you have learned the most from the reading?
  - How does this remind you of other readings?
  - Does this book make you think of yourself or anything else? How?
  - Do you want to read more of the same kind of books? Why yes or no?
- Journal writing (help students move away from daily list recording, students may write in Chinese, but encourage them to write as much English as possible)
  - What is the most important thing on your mind recently?
  - Anything that makes you happy.
  - Anything that bothers you.
  - Anything on your mind all the time.
  - Tell something you miss the most in China.
  - Tell something you like and/or dislike in America.
- Writing assignment for CLA class
  - You can do this writing only in English in this class.

Group 4: The Group That Works with the Teacher (a variety of activities the teacher chooses based on students' language and reading level and their needs)

- Shared reading with the teacher: if this is a group of very beginning learners, choose one or two books students have practiced reading at home or listened to in the listening center. Big books would be better.
  - Ask students if they have any questions about the book.
  - Lead them to read once or twice.

- Help them pronounce the words or sounds they have the most difficulty with.
- Let students memorize the repetitive part on each page and recall the text without looking at the words (cover that part on each page).
- Work out with the students a list of vocabulary words that can replace the words in the sentence patterns and create a new text.
- Have students read the new text until they can say it without looking at the words.
- Teach or review relevant language skills they need to create the new story, such as plural forms and pronouns.
- Let students write new stories on their own or in pairs (before you leave them for another group).
- Literature study with the teacher: if this group is able to read picture books or chapter books, choose a book they have read at home.
  - Read the book together with the students to set the mood.
  - Ask students what they have learned from the book.
  - Ask students about their questions or the parts they find difficult.
  - Reread the parts they find difficult and have a discussion based on the content.
  - Through discussion, discover the issues that students have an interest in or are concerned with, and lead an in-depth discussion on those issues.
  - Then move the content discussion to the language used, writing styles, and certain writing elements.
  - Any relevant reading, writing, or inquiry projects that can further their learning should be extended activities.
- Minilessons on writing with the group:
  - Model different ways to write reading responses.
  - Describe journal writing that is more meaningful and interesting.
  - Introduce writer's notebook.
  - Use a book as a model to talk about writing techniques the author used.
  - Give a minilesson on peer editing and language skills.
  - Prepare students for publishing their writing.
  - Work with students on their inquiry or research projects.

I asked the teachers to see these group activities as possibilities, but not as teaching manuals. They needed to alter them according to their knowledge of their own students and their learning progress. The students should be grouped not only according to their abilities but also according to their interests and needs.

One of the challenges in teaching multiple groups is groupwork design. Traditionally, teaching in small groups means only teaching a short lesson to one small group at a time and giving the rest of the class seatwork. The purpose of the seatwork is often to keep the students busy or occupied so as to free the teacher to work with one small group at a time. When the teacher takes a group, the work is often disconnected from what they have done previously on their own. Students either don't take their seatwork seriously or have to discontinue their independent work when the teacher comes to them. For instance, in one class, a group of the students were sent to the listening center to listen to a book on tape. Ten minutes later, when the teacher worked with them, she did a shared reading with a different book. She didn't check what the students did in the listening center or ask if they had any questions about the book they had just practiced reading and listening to. Furthermore, their small-group activity should be closely linked with what the teacher does with them before and after. This means when students work in their own small group, they either prepare or review for the lesson that the teacher gives.

Colleen, an ESL seventh-grade teacher, worked hard to improve the cohesiveness in her teaching with multiple groups. When working in small groups on their own, her students either reviewed what they had learned or prepared to work with her when it was their turn. She gave each group specific directions and told them what she expected them to accomplish. When she took the group, she would check their previous work and then work on the questions or problems they had. Sometimes she had to send the group back to continue working on their own again if she found they had not accomplished what they were supposed to do.

I observed how Colleen worked with one group specifically. This was an independent reading group with six students. She gave them each *Snowing Day* by Ezra Jack Keats with the following directions:

- Go through the book first to learn the story from the pictures.
- Read with a dictionary.
- Write down questions you have.
- Work with a partner to discuss your questions.
- Write down the remaining questions.

Fifteen minutes later, when she worked with this group, she started with the questions the students brought up. Instead of giving them answers, she directed the students to reread certain pages and have a discussion after their reading. During this time, she left the group for a few minutes to check other groups' work and then came back to continue the book discussion with this group. In this way, not only were the students prepared for the lesson she planned to teach to this group, but also the students' questions revealed what she should teach or focus on, rather than working through the text line by line and asking questions page to page as she used to do. The students knew exactly what they should do and worked seriously in small groups on their own. She had excellent time control when she worked with each group. It took almost a year for her to have a good grip on the flow of the groupwork, and then she became the school's model in teaching multiple groups.

Time Management in Teaching Multiple Groups

Time management and finding reading materials on the same topic for students with various levels of English ability present another challenge. Pam and I worked very hard with the teachers, especially the newly hired ones, on class management. Pam searched through catalogs and ordered books of different genres and varieties in terms of topics and language levels for every classroom. Now in the school, every classroom has a library with hundreds of books, including many collections of big books and tapes, each with multiple copies.

Nikoleta, a new ESL teacher, experimented with small-group teaching with multiple levels of books in reading instruction. It took her a few months to feel comfortable and get into the right rhythm. Of her twenty students, six could read English only at a simple sentence level with limited English vocabulary, nine students could read picture books at the second- or third-grade level, and five could read simple chapter books. To meet all her students' needs, she grouped her class into ability groups when she was teaching the genre of biography. Nikoleta found books at various language levels on a variety of the topics related to historical figures like George Washington, Abraham Lincoln, and Martin Luther King Jr. For the lessons on George Washington, she gave the very beginners group books of photographs with captions. The two middle-level groups were given picture books (fiction or nonfiction) of George Washington, and the advanced group had simple nonfiction chapter books in the middle of the table. Prior to the lesson, she asked the class what they knew about George Washington and what they wanted to know about him (KWL strategy). She worked with them in asking significant questions and avoiding unimportant ones like "How many children did he have?" She wrote what the students said on the easel and listed all their questions. When the students gave her Chinese, she would ask other students to translate it and she put the English words down. After class, her students took the books home for reading homework. The beginners group was also given books on tape for listening and reading practice.

The next day, the class was grouped according to three levels of ability. The middle-level groups would work in pairs using the information they had read at home to answer the questions listed the previous day. The advanced group would write independently about what they had learned about Washington. The teacher would work with the beginners group first. With the homework reading, the students were prepared for what they were expected to do. Nikoleta spent the first fifteen minutes with the beginners group, checking their understanding and leading them to read the captions and talk more about the photos of Washington and his life. Before she left the first group, she paired the students so that they could read to each other and practice talking about pictures without reading the captions.

Then she worked with the middle-level groups to see if they had learned enough information to answer the questions raised by the class or if they had found that they had any incorrect information about Washington before their reading. Before she took off to the last group, she asked the students each to write a paragraph on what they had learned about Washington. With the advanced group, she had each student share his or her writing with the group and she and other group members gave feedback and asked more questions.

Time management was an issue in teaching multiple groups. We worked hard with Nikoleta on how to give each group enough work to keep them busy until she could get to them and how to assign the students appropriate work that they could do independently. It was very easy to work overtime with one group and not to leave enough time for the others. In my first demonstration lesson, I had barely enough time to get to the last group and had a hard time keeping the groups working independently for more than twenty minutes. That lesson made me realize that it was very hard to spend fifteen minutes evenly with each group in a forty-five minute lesson. Within fifteen minutes, the teacher had to give the students enough help to enable them to work for thirty minutes on their own.

Nikoleta solved this problem skillfully. She would work with a group for five to ten minutes, then let them do some quick reading or writing for five to ten minutes. During this time, she would check with other groups and help them with the questions they had. Then she would come back to the first group and continue to work with them until she could leave them for ten to fifteen minutes for independent work. It took a lot of practice for Nikoleta to get the flow and the right rhythm. To challenge each group appropriately, Nikoleta had the groups give different presentations at the end of the unit on George Washington. The students in the beginners group each gave a one- or two-sentence presentation of Washington while holding a photo in their hands. The students in the middle-level groups presented in pairs what they learned about Washington and what made him a great leader and man. The students from the advanced group were required to give supplementary information about Washington that was not included in the presentations given by the other groups. In these presentations, the students of different levels all participated and also were appropriately challenged. And the whole class learned more about George Washington from each other's presentations.

It was a rewarding experience for every student. But by the end, the students somewhat lost concentration or were not as interested in listening to their peers, especially when the content of the presentation became quite repetitive among the members in the same group. To solve this problem, I suggested that Nikoleta regroup students from different levels into one group and have students present in small groups rather than to the whole class. This way, we could have three or four students present at the same time to a smaller audience and have the same effect of learning from different perspectives in less time. Nikoleta liked my idea and tried it when the class presented their study of Martin Luther King Jr. In order to let each group feel equally important, she invited Alice, Pam, and other adults in the building to join the group presentations.

Finally, I convinced her that she didn't have to read every book she asked her students to read, especially all the chapter books for the advanced group. We had to learn to trust students, let them teach us what they had learned, and accept the fact that we couldn't know everything. Students got excited when they found they could teach the teacher something new, and as Nancie Atwell discussed in her book *In the Middle* (1998), more authentic book talk took place between the teacher and the students when the teacher didn't read the book. In a real book discussion, instead of checking the students' reading comprehension, we ask real questions and show our real curiosity toward what our students say about their books. But for a teacher to accept a learning stance in front of her students, she not only needs confidence but also needs to believe that teaching is not simply delivering information and that real learning happens in the process of interaction.

Other Issues Related to Small-Group Work

With the most basic beginners class, the teachers tended to divide the students according to their language or reading abilities, as Nikoleta did for her lesson on George Washington. In a class with more advanced English proficiency, the teachers were able to group the students according to their interests and needs. Betty grouped her sixth-grade ESL class according to the countries they liked to study when teaching the Countries in the World unit. She had an Italy group, a Japan group, a Mexico group, a Korea group, and an India group. These groups included students with varying levels of English proficiency and academic ability. In each group, the students would read books about their country, do research to find more information, and present their learning in their published books as a group. In Marci's seventh-grade class, when studying the rain forest, her students were grouped according to their choice of animals. By the end of the unit, each group had a considerable depth of knowledge about the animal they chose to study and the whole class learned a great deal from the group presentations and group-published nonfiction books. Working with each small group, Betty and Marci helped their students read, research, write, revise, publish, and present their work.

Now in the ESL classes, the teachers often integrate the whole-class and small-group teaching in a lesson. We rarely see any teachers give a whole-class lesson for the entire class period. The teachers usually spend the first five or ten minutes reading aloud, doing daily news or giving directions or teaching a minilesson to the whole class. Then they divide the students into small groups, sometimes with different books for each group or different activities related to the same book. Roza adopted the idea of the literature circle for reading instruction. When her class started to read a new book, the students would get into four different groups:

- Vocabulary Enricher: In this group, each student would choose five unknown words, find the definitions, and teach the words to the group.

- Passage Picker: In this group, each student would find four interesting, surprising, or significant passages and share them with the group.

- Illustrator: In this group, each student would draw a favorite scene from her understanding of the book and explain her drawing to the group.

- Quotation Chooser: In this group, each student would choose five quotes and ask the group to identify the speakers.

For each group, one discussion director would be chosen to lead the discussion, take notes, and ask questions. The group director would then report their groupwork to the class before rotating to one of the other group activities. The students seemed to enjoy the literature circles very much. When working in his or her small group, every student had an opportunity to read, talk, share, and teach. Roza became an expert in using this strategy and presented her work several times at the faculty workshops.

The newcomers and students with limited English proficiency not only need to learn language skills but also need to learn how to learn. "To ask your own questions," and "to express what you know," and "to write a personal response" all may sound very foreign to those students. As a foreign student in this country, I learned the most from observing how my peers learned and how they responded to the teacher's requests and from listening to how others voiced their opinions and shared their thoughts. How they presented their views was equally important as what they said. I believe that for the sake of our students' learning, we should group our students according to their interests and needs more than according to their abilities, even though it is easier to teach when students are tracked by levels. Our students need to learn new knowledge and skills not only from the teacher but also from each other.

In small groups, students get more chances to talk among themselves and with the teacher. For ESL students, especially for our Chinese students who are not used to sharing their thoughts in public, talking in small groups is a good place to start. But it can also be a problem for some Chinese students to work in small groups. In China, the students are often trained to passively listen to the teacher and to take only the teacher's words seriously. They come to school ready to listen to the teachers, but not to their peers. Groupwork, peer conferencing, and sharing can be foreign concepts to many Chinese students. They are not used to sharing their thinking with their peers or being questioned or challenged by their peers. When our students were first asked to work with their peers in small groups, many of them wouldn't take the group discussion seriously and many wouldn't listen to their peers. Some either fooled around, did minimum work, or sat there waiting for the teacher if they had questions. It took time for them to learn to work with peers, to believe they and their peers had valuable ideas to offer, to share their work, and to interact with others. Very often, when we see our new Chinese students unable to work well in groups, we tend to think it is only because of their language barriers. It is much more. When they learn a new language, they are learning a new way of learning, new concepts, and new values behind the target language.

I remember when I first came to study in America, I resented small-group work. I thought that working with peers in class was a waste of time, thinking that I paid to get knowledge from the teacher, but not from the people that were not much better than me. Though I didn't mind working with my peers outside of class, I didn't value their ideas or opinions and refused to consider their responses in my writing, as I didn't believe they would hold the same standard as the teacher. Of course, I didn't believe in my own words or thinking, either. It took me years before I could really appreciate interactive ways of learning and learned to value both my peers' and my own views and opinions.

Now when I see some Chinese students who don't take the groupwork seriously, I recall my own first experiences in this country and believe that there may be more reasons than just them "being less motivated or lazy." I think that providing specific instructions and expectations for groupwork helps the new Chinese immigrant students adjust better to their small-group work than simply assigning them an activity such as "Do buddy reading" or "Share your response in groups," which may confuse them in some way, especially when only new language beginners are grouped together.

From working with the teachers on their experiments with multiple groups, I have realized what enables teaching multiple groups to be successful:

- Know your students' ability and language levels, their needs, and their interests.

- Build a classroom library with sets of books of different levels on the same topic and theme and with books on tape (both teacher-made and commercial).

- Give specific instructions and expectations for every group assignment (model when necessary).

- Set different goals for different ability groups, and have each group present their learning at their level.

- Check students' work to see if they met the goals or expectations, and help them with their questions before you start something new when you work with a small group.

- Be flexible with groupwork time. If one group needs more time to work in their small group, they should be allowed that time.

- Try to have two periods back-to-back for solid groupwork.

- Give students time to learn to work with each other and to learn to depend on each other to learn.

- Require every student to participate in the group presentation.

- Group students according to their needs and interests, not only their abilities.

Teaching with multiple groups is not a new idea to our teachers, but to get it right takes time and effort.

Helping Newcomers and Struggling Students Catch Up

In addition to small-group teaching, buddy reading, peer tutoring, and group collaboration are other ways our teachers tried teaching the students with a wide range of language abilities. These strategies are not only good for helping the students who need the most help but are also good for helping them get to know their peers. But we should avoid always pairing advanced students with the students with very limited English proficiency. The advanced students may feel they are not being challenged or inspired, but rather that they are being used. And the beginners may sense their tutors' impatience, so they may feel stupid and humiliated. In some of our ESL classes, I found quite a few students reluctantly admitting that they could speak Chinese or Fuzhou dialect because, as they stated, they were tired of being always assigned to work with the newcomers; "I don't want just to help others to learn; I want to learn myself."

We should give all the students, not just a few, opportunities to help newcomers. This gives each of them a chance to get to know the new students. When we assign our students to do buddy reading or peer tutoring, we should have a specific purpose: to help, to share, to model, to practice reading, or to review a newly learned skill with each other. With different purposes, we pair a student with different partners who we think will be the most compatible. As a matter of fact, the students who are close to the newcomer's level could be the best tutors. They can practice or teach what they have just learned and also explain a newly acquired skill to a partner.

I was fascinated by a buddy reading session in which one student who came to the United States just a few months earlier helped a student who arrived only a few days before my visit. They were reading a pattern book. The more skilled reader pointed at each line, reading word by word, and then asked the new student to read after him. When the new student had a hard time pronouncing a word or a sound, the tutor would show the tutee where to put his tongue to pronounce /l/ or /r/ or how to stretch the sound for *bird* or *lake*. Sometimes the tutor would stop at a word that he could not read and look up to me for help. When I taught him, he would immediately turn to teach it to his tutee. Then they both would try to get it right by speaking the word many times to each other. It is this tutor who taught me that a student like him can be the best teacher for the student who is just a step behind him.

We tend to water down our curriculum and give less work to the struggling students than to the rest of the class. We assume that we shouldn't frustrate them or overwhelm them, as they are not able to handle the work like the rest of the class. Actually, the struggling students and newcomers need to do more in order to catch up. I do not mean they need to catch up with the rest of the class or even to try to reach their grade level based upon a certain standard. That may not be possible in many cases. What I do mean is that we should give these students more rather than fewer chances to learn both in and outside of school. Students, especially our middle school–aged ones, can do much learning on their own. We should help them by teaching them how to practice listening and speaking with a tape recorder at home and by assigning them reading or writing homework every day to prepare for the next day's class. Coming to class without any or less preparation than others makes it harder for the newcomers and struggling students to participate in class. I learned from my Chinatown friends that quite a number of new Chinese immigrants sent their newly arrived children to the English tutoring programs in Chinatown after school or during the weekend to catch up with their schoolwork. But most of the students who have problems with their schoolwork don't have this opportunity and they have to depend solely on their school. If we can enrich their time outside the classroom by teaching them how they can learn on their own or how their families can help, the students will learn more quickly.

Once when I was working with a new ESL student in a class, I found new ESL students could do more than we expected. I was observing a math lesson and was sitting in the back with a student who came to America a few months earlier. I explained to him a math problem the teacher was teaching and helped him with his work. Before the class ended, the teacher was giving the students homework, and he, as a newcomer, received a different set of homework from the others. I showed him the set of homework for the others and asked him if he could do it. He nodded his head and said that his cousin could help him with the work. When I asked him to take it home and try to do the same homework as the others, he shook his head, saying, "No, I don't want my teacher to know, and I don't mind getting the easier work." Children, after all, are children. They want to take the easy route when they can. This incident told me that we should give the students more challenging work than we think they can handle to see where their potential is. If they can get help outside for the work, that is an extra learning opportunity for them. I told the teacher what I found out from the boy, and later he received the same homework as the others, and the teacher told him to do as much as he could. He managed to do all the work with the help from his cousin, who was two grades above him.

This example brings to light a controversial issue related to the purpose of homework. Many teachers believe that students should do their homework independently, saying, "How do we know a student understands the materials if he or she gets help from the family?" This question is valid. But there is a difference between a student being helped with homework and letting others do her homework. The latter is wrong. But we cannot take a learning opportunity away from all students just because some are not doing things right. If we let students collaborate and help each other in class, why not let them continue this practice at home?

Teaching students in a class with a wide range of language abilities is very challenging. The teachers in IS 131 continue to search for effective ways to help all the students learn as much as possible when they are at school. They give each other ideas and present their successes at the faculty workshops.

At the beginning when we first tried to teach with multiple groups and multiple books, it was very hard. Now our teachers have gained much experience and support from each other, and they contain in their classrooms quite an extensive collection of books and books on tape at different language levels on the same themes or topics. They feel much more confident, comfortable, and also more prepared to teach students with a wide range of language or reading abilities. They have not stopped learning new ways and they often encounter and solve new problems. Sometimes, in late spring, new students come to their classrooms with idiosyncratic learning styles; the teachers have to readjust their teaching methods or style to suit the new students' needs. That is teaching: challenging and interesting, with no fixed format.

5

Teaching Beginning ESL Writers

When talking about helping beginning ESL students write, I am often confronted with the following questions:

- How can we help ESL students write when they are just beginning to develop their basic language skills?

- Should we wait until those students have developed their reading and speaking skills before teaching them to write?

- How can they start to write when they barely know their ABCs?

Since Alice became the principal of IS 131, writing has been emphasized in the school and the search for the best method to teach writing to ESL students has never ceased among the literacy faculty. This has become a most interesting, challenging, and exciting experience for all of us; we have learned more about our students—and about teaching writing to students with little to no English proficiency. But there are no absolute keys to those puzzles.

Now all students in IS 131 are required, encouraged, and helped to write from the first week they arrive in the classrooms, no matter how limited their English proficiency. When Maureen was helping the teachers teach more writing and rely less on worksheets in their teaching, she suggested reading such authors as Shelley Harwayne, Linda Rief, and Nancie Atwell and introduced various types of writing into classrooms. She demonstrated poetry teaching and reading and writing connections ("*Change My Life Forever,*" Barbieri 2002). When I came, I joined her in searching for effective methods to help beginning ESL students learn to write. Ever since, writing has become a major focus in every classroom. In this chapter, I will share how our teachers helped our beginning English language learners grow as writers and develop their literacy and language skills through writing.

Writing in Their First Language

In the teaching of writing to emergent writers, we encourage students to write how they speak. This includes allowing them to use invented spelling to express their ideas before they learn how to spell the words needed in their writing. But our beginning ESL students don't have their oral language as a base for their English writing, so it is impossible for them to use the invented spelling strategy to write. However, what they do have is their primary language. All our Chinese new immigrant students can speak Chinese properly, and most of them can write and read, even though many may not be at their grade level. In order to continue their overall writing development, I encouraged our teachers to let the students read and write in Chinese before they could do so in English. I believe thinking (reasoning and imagination) and the ability to organize ideas are equally, or even more, important than language skills in learning to write. If we let our students express themselves and present their ideas in their primary language, we give them opportunities to continue the development of their thinking. With this development uninterrupted, they are able to write well in a second language once they develop proficiency in it. If we let them wait until their English is good enough, their thinking and writing skills will not only have stopped developing but will have diminished—especially damaging for those students who don't yet have good writing skills in their first language.

Shirley, a seventh-grade ESL teacher, shared: "At first, I didn't let them [the students in the beginners class] speak or write in Chinese, but only in English. They couldn't write or speak up. They refused to talk. Then I let them use Chinese. They began to speak and write more, or write in mixed language. Now [in the spring] they write mostly in English with a few Chinese words, but their writing is very Chinese English." Shirley thought, as I did before, that by forbidding her students to use Chinese in the ESL learning, she would speed up their English learning, but soon she realized that didn't work. Through working with Chinese students for many years, all our CLA teachers realized that those students who can write well in Chinese learn English faster and write better in English once they learn the language.

All our students are given time to write each day in class from the first week they arrive, either in ESL or CLA classes, despite how proficient their English is and how recently they arrived in the United States. Susan, a sixth-grade ESL teacher, had twenty-seven brand-new students in her class, some of whom had been in America for only a few days. During my visit, I saw the students working in three groups: six at the listening center listening to the book *From Head to Toe* by Eric Carle; one group of six with Susan doing shared reading of *Brown Bear, Brown Bear, What Do You See?* by Bill Martin Jr. and Eric Carle; and the rest of the class silently reading books written either in Chinese or in bilingual languages (Chinese and English) or writing in their journals.

Susan doesn't understand Chinese. When I asked her how she checked her students' Chinese writing, she responded: "I just check if they wrote, how much they wrote, but not what they wrote. I wish I could, but I assume as long as they read and write, they will continue to develop their skills as readers and writers. Sometimes I ask them to illustrate what they wrote. From the pictures, I could guess the basic content of their stories." Susan is not just keeping the students occupied with Chinese reading and writing; she understands that their reading and writing in Chinese will help them develop their English reading and writing skills.

In Betty's sixth-grade beginning ESL class, she had her students write in their reading journals every day. They took English books home to read with dictionaries and each made his or her own Chinese-English dictionary. They started to read simple pattern books (one sentence on each page) and later moved to high-level pattern books (with three or four sentences on each page). By November, many of them could read simple picture storybooks. After reading, they had to write a reading journal in Chinese every night. At first, they would draw a picture and write a caption underneath. Later, when their reading had more complicated plots, they would draw a group of pictures with captions (see Figure 5–1). Betty explained her purpose for these journal entries: "I want to make sure they read every night and they understand their reading. And also, I want them to form a habit of reading and learn to write reading responses."

When her students started to read picture storybooks, Betty modeled how to write reading summaries and responses. She modeled to her English beginners how to make personal as well as text-to-text connections in the reading responses. Being bilingual herself, Betty was able to teach and respond to her students' writing in Chinese. In addition, from very early on, Betty pushed her students to insert any English words they knew into their Chinese writing. She read their reading responses every day and pushed them in every piece to include the English words they knew in their writing (see Figure 5–2). She believed: "By allowing them to write in Chinese and also pushing them to write as much English as they can, I helped them learn how to write reading responses and at the same time helped them develop their English skills— learn to use the English words they learned in a context. In three months, many started to write their responses in all English."

The students wrote frequently in CLA class. All our English beginners had to attend CLA class, where they developed their reading and writing skills mostly in Chinese through learning about America. With each CLA teacher having 100 to 120 students, he or she could barely work with the students

Figure 5–1 A Group of Pictures as Reading Response

individually. Requiring frequent reading and writing was the only way to develop the students' reading and writing skills in the CLA class. During an interview, Jian explained how he helped his students develop their writing skills:

> I have my students write two pieces each week, mostly essays. Many students never learned how to write essays in the Western way in China, so I have to model how to write essays, like with an introduction and a conclusion. I showed them many examples and worked with the whole class for

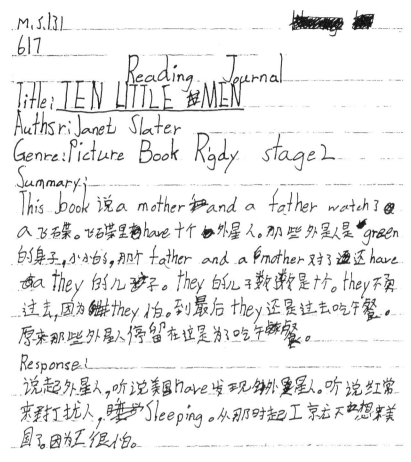

Figure 5–2 A Reading Response in Chinese Mixed with English Words

the first few weeks, then most students would eventually get it. About 20 percent would always have problems. They are probably at third- or fourth-grade level in their Chinese, and now they are in eighth grade. Both the content and writing requirement are hard for those students. I spread those students in each group and pair them with strong students each. I wish I could work with those struggling students individually more. But with 115 students, and with such a heavy content I have to cover, I hardly have any time to work with the individuals. What I could do is to give those students more writing samples to follow. Each year, I keep some good students' writing samples and use them as writing models. Sometimes, I talk to them while others are working in groups. But I hate to take them out of group discussion because it is important for them to hear their peers. I also pair the struggling students with strong students. Before they turn in any work, they have to give it to their partner to check it. I give those helpers some extra credits. With writing frequently in this way, the struggling students gradually develop their writing skills. Now they can write at least three paragraphs cohesively, while the others can write three pages.

Through producing two pieces each week in their CLA class throughout the year, all of the students developed their writing skills gradually. Their continuous growth as writers in their first language will help a great deal when they are able to write in English.

Writing in their first language not only provides them with opportunities to continue to develop their writing and thinking skills but also gives us a chance to understand them as literate persons or a channel through which to reach them as individuals, which their current limited English proficiency doesn't enable us to do. I happened to read a piece written in Chinese by a new student whose English was very limited. His writings in Chinese have made me reach a profound understanding of all the Chinese students like him. This piece is titled "The Unforgetable Day."

> The first day of a person's new life in a new world would always be unforgetable memory.
>
> Four months ago, I boarded the airplane to America, to my new homeland. Filled with all the hope and excitement, I was approaching America, my new world. But I was sad, and feeling lost at the same time as the airplane took me farther and farther away from the land where I was born, and the people who took care of me since my birth. It was so hard to leave behind all my families and friends. The fact of not knowing when to see them again hurt me terribly.
>
> We arrived in New York at night. I looked down at the city. Wow, this is America! Its streets and gigantic buildings were all brightly lit. My heart was lifted up as if the lights lit up my body too. I saw cars endlessly running through the street like a lantern-lit river or a fire dragon. Every building was tall and beautiful, and the lights made it look so magnificent. I saw the American suspended bridge, with cars running on the top and trains going through in the middle. All these incredible views excited me, and gave me great hope and expectation for America.
>
> On the way to my new home, it started to rain; the raindrops hit the car windows, and blocked the view outside. I quietly dropped into thought of my home, my families, and my friends in China, what we did together, as if I heard us playing and laughing together. It was like a movie. I missed them so much at that moment.
>
> When we arrived at our apartment building, I was shocked. When we walked into the apartment, I was shocked even more. I couldn't believe my eyes: the room was tiny and old. I thought it was only the living room, but

my mom told me this was all we had. At that moment, all my hope and excitement for America was shattered. This building was as old as the wood
storage we had in China, and the whole apartment was just like a sitting
room at home. I didn't have my own room, and my bed was the tiny one in
the corner. While my parents were unpacking my luggage, my aunt was
telling me about their life in America. I was led to face the truth.

That was a very unforgetable day for me. I felt sad, homesick and loss
for all I had in China. I saw the magnificnt view of America, but I realized
my life in this land had nothing to do with those magnificent lights, skylight
buildings, endless running cars, and suspended bridge. I went through all
kinds of feelings and thoughts in one day, but I could never forget the
American lights.

Writing in their first language enabled these new immigrant students to
express what was deep in their hearts and helped them make the transition
into this new world, but it also gave them a personal meaning for their school
learning. But this student, like many, was not able to do so in his English
writing. The following is one of his daily journals that he wrote in English:

This morning I mother said, tomorrow go to the uncle home eat lunch. I am
very happy. Because I am like to uncle home, morning, I watch News T.V.
Yesterday I am very happy. Yesterday, I third teacher absent. The yesterday
is no home worle.

Contrasting what this student was able to write in English and in Chinese, I
realized more how important it was to let the students write in their first
language. His limited English proficiency didn't allow him to demonstrate his
real literacy or express his ideas. Letting new immigrant students write in their
first language has given them a chance to continue to develop their thinking
and literacy skills and an opportunity to express themselves and search for
their new identities, and it has also been a channel for us to understand them
as individuals.

Having Freedom in Their Writing Styles

In our English beginners classes, by November, we begin to see the students
write in different language styles, which often represent their different stages
as English language learners. Some write only in Chinese, some in Chinese
with a few English words and phrases, some in English with Chinese words
here and there, some in Chinese English, which is English words in Chinese
syntax, and still others in nearly Standard English (see Figures 5–3a and b).
These stages of writing development demonstrate the students' progress in
their English language learning. It is similar to the way people learn to speak
in English as a second language: They have to speak their first language before

Writing in Chinese mixed with English

Writing in Chinese

Figure 5–3a Stages of Chinese ESL Students' Writing Development

Writing in English with Chinese syntax and expressions

"My friend in America"
in my school still this and my very good friend. He is my in school pass January only friend. in school he and me inseparable. friend. We is same class schoolmate. he name is Li yal. he English compare good. My incapable make homework time. Li you teach my make homework. go home, Li you and my piece play basketbal. every day we city piece go play. Sometimes we play electron. sometimes we be park play sport. we be piece very happy. he is my best friend

Writing in acceptable English close to Standard English

I like china, because in the china I have many friends. we are play football, in Somer. we are Swimming Swiming. but in the American I only have four friends, I dont know where are their homes; they don't know where is my home is

I like china, because in china, everyone speak Chinese, I can understand. But in the America, American people all speak English. I don't understand. If I can speak English, I like America too, now, I wish is I can speak English, because I like America too, so, I must learn English.

Figure 5–3b

they can express themselves in English. Later, they mix a few English words in their talk. After they study English intensively for a while, they speak English mixed with some words from the first language. Gradually, they try to speak English, but they still think in their first language, so their speech tends to sound very foreign, such as Chinese English. With much practice in English listening and speaking, they develop their speech in Standard English. This gradual development in English speaking occurs on the condition that the learners never stop speaking and intentionally try to use English as much as possible in their speech.

In our ESL and CLA classes, our students develop their writing skills in the same way people develop their English-speaking ability. They never stop writing. Once they learn some English—either individual words, phrases, or some simple sentences—they are encouraged to utilize them in their writing. Our teachers are used to reading their students' writing in different language styles and have learned to look through the facade to get to the meanings. Most of our ESL teachers cannot read or write in Chinese, so they check their students' work as Susan described earlier. They check their students' actions and efforts: if they wrote and how much they wrote, rather than the content and quality of their writing. When the students write more English than Chinese, teachers can guess the meaning of their writing and carry on a conference with the writers. Bilingual teachers like Betty, John, and Shirley were able to push their students very hard in developing their writing skills in both Chinese and English. Because these bilingual teachers are able to help the beginning ESL students write in both Chinese and English, they are often assigned to teach the beginning ESL classes.

Our teachers let students choose the way they wanted to write at any time. Our ESL teachers showed their students examples of writing with different language styles and encouraged them to use English whenever they could, but their writing was never graded based on how much English they used in their work. Newcomers usually started to write in Chinese. One or two months later, they would insert English words and phrases in their writing (Betty's students started to do this during the second week in her class) because it was natural for them to do so when they were immersed in English learning every day with reading, writing, listening, and speaking activities.

In CLA class, though the students usually did more writing in Chinese, many of them also took any opportunity to practice writing in English whenever they could. Most of them did their assignments in CLA classes in two mixed languages, such as the work in their notebooks, the posters on the walls, the papers they turned in, and their classroom publications. In the spring of 2000, the hallway of Jian's sixth-grade class displayed the students' works on the topic of spring written in four different styles: in all English; in English mixed with Chinese words; in bilingual languages (parallel Chinese and English); and in all Chinese, such as the following four examples:

Example 1: Spring (written in English)

Spring is very beautiful. It is very warm when spring comes. The farmers plant the vegetable in the farm. The animals come out from spring and come out to get food. There is much fresh water in the mountain. And the air smells very fresh. When it was in China and it is spring I always go to the mountain to play or go the swimming. But in America when it is spring I was in school. When spring come it make me feel cheerful. Everyday I weak up I see the sun shine at me. Many animals were born in the spring. I wish every day were spring.

Example 2: Spring (English mixed with Chinese words)

Spring is the first 季节 of a year, the spring make the mother earth. When the spring was come there have the beautiful flowers and the 翠绿啟 tree and it also have the 快乐 birds come back to our city, and everyday we can hear the bird singing and the cat dancing and dog 蹦蹦跳跳 . When we go outside we can 眺望着 the tree and the flower that 迎风摆摆 are in the sky and the spring make us very happy.

Example 3: 春天/Spring (bilingual)

在春天, 那美麗的花來, 孩子他們也在公園
玩, 人人穿著衣服也變成夏少的 , 多數的鳥
也飛來, 天空也變成藍色當時的時間真正的熱的, 那
天空的太陽真正的熱的, 美麗的花來蝴蝶 也飛
來 , 人人 快樂的去玩, 學校也 放孩子他們不
去學校,

When the spring is come the beautiful flowers are come and the children who play in the park to play and the people who wear the less clothes and many birds come and the school are close and children who do not go to school and people who was very happy that are go to play because in summer people who play in the beach.

Example 4: Spring (my translation from Chinese; see Figure 5–4 for the original)

Spring is here. Everywhere is filled with new life. In the morning, I wake up and open my eyes, see the whole earth as if it were just opening its eyes and waking up like me, fresh and energetic. Water fills up the lake, where fish swim back and forth as if they are announcing: "Spring is here. Spring is here."

I walk by some apple trees. They are standing straight on the ground, with leaves washed clean without any dust by the spring shower.

I walk further and pass by some willow trees by the lake. They are also showered by the spring rain, with dustless leaves and shining green buds. Their branches wave in the warm spring wind, as if they are dancing to welcome the coming of spring.

In the lake, there are beautiful lotus flowers, which are wearing a pretty hat. Frogs are jumping back and forth among the flowers, as if they are happily dancing.

I walk farther and arrive at the traveling road. From there, I look up, seeing vast green rice field, where farmers are busy planting at this time of the year, Spring.

Then I continue to walk, and walk into the edgeless woods. The trees there have a green and healthy look after being rinsed by the spring showers.

My final walk takes me to a village, where houses are dusted by spring shower as if they are newly built.

Oh, Spring is so beautiful!

I love Spring.

But I love even more the beauty and life Spring brings to us.

According to the teacher, the students who chose to write in Chinese were not necessarily weaker in their English skills than the students who chose to write in English. Some students who were able to write in English in their reading responses and writer's notebooks would sometimes choose to write in Chinese for certain assignments. Their choice depended upon topics or the content they had to write. The writer of the piece shown in Figure 5–4 was unable to produce the same quality in English with his current limited English proficiency. His English skills, according to his teacher, were at a similar level with many others who chose to write this assignment in English. When we evaluate ESL students' writing, we tend to judge their English ability based on how much they can write in English. Now from these students' work, I have realized that our adjustment might not be accurate, and my analysis of the stages of ESL writing could sometimes be artificial, rigid, or even oversimplistic.

CLA

Spring

春天到来了，大地到处都充满了生气。早晨，我刚刚下床，睁开眼睛一看，一切都好像刚刚睡醒是似的，欣欣然，张开了眼。河里的水涨得满满的。小鱼在水里游来游去，好像在说："春天到来了，春天到来了!"

走过一些，一棵棵苹果树挺立在地面上，苹果树上的叶子经过春雨的清洗后，叶子显得一尘不染。

再走过一些，湖边的柳树也经过春雨的清洗后，叶子也一尘不染。柳树的枝上长出绿油油的枝条。一阵春风吹来，把柳树吹得一摆一摆，好像在欢迎春天的到来而遍遍地舞。

湖里的荷花长得非常美丽，像一顶顶帽子那样，湖里的青蛙在荷花里蹦来跳去，好像在开心地跳舞。

又走过一些，到马路上，一眼看去是绿油油的稻田，走过春天的农民都忙忙碌碌地插秧。

再走过一些，是一望无际的森林，森林里的树苗在春雨的冲洗下长得非常之绿和非常茂盛。

再走过一些，是一条村庄，村庄的屋在春雨的冲洗下，变得一尘不染像刚刚建成的。

啊! 春天真美呀!

我爱春天。

我更爱春天的景色。

Figure 5–4 A Piece of Chinese Writing About Spring

I was glad that our students were given the freedom to choose the way and the language they would write in, or they would have suffered limitations in presenting themselves. I found this to be true when I read through students' portfolios, in which the selected pieces were arranged chronologically. In the portfolios, there was a variety of writing samples, including reading responses, personal narratives, essay presentations, summaries of reading, charts, and graphs. They were written in the various styles, as shown earlier. The works written in English were not the most recent products but usually were short pieces with simple content; however, the lengthy pieces, which presented more complicated ideas, tended to be written in Chinese. I began to realize that it was the topic or the complexity of a piece of writing that determined what language our students chose to use in their writing. This shows that our students were able to use language freely as a tool to express themselves and they knew what language they needed for what topics and how they would like to present themselves as writers. As thinkers and writers, our students are given the kind of freedom that students usually don't have when they are learning to write in a new language. With the opportunity this freedom provides, I find our English language beginners not only have few limitations as student writers but also can express themselves freely in writing when they barely know their ABCs, or when they are just beginning to develop their basic English language skills.

Creating Their Own Pattern Books

Pattern book writing is the first type of writing our beginning ESL students do purely in English. In the same way as we develop our beginners' English language skills in their oral language and reading, we use pattern books to develop their English writing skills. Writing development parallels oral language development. From reading and listening to pattern books, our students learn English grammar and vocabulary in the repetitive sentences in meaningful contexts. Creating their own pattern books, our students not only review their newly learned knowledge but also apply it to a new context.

For instance, here's the repetitive pattern in *Brown Bear, Brown Bear, What Do You See?*

Brown Bear,
Brown Bear,
What do you see?
I see a red bird looking at me.
Red Bird,
Red Bird,
What do you see?
I see a yellow duck looking at me.

After the students fluently read these patterns, the teacher helps them work out an original pattern with different vocabulary, and they produce a different book with the same pattern orally as a class. Then the students have a similar writing assignment. An example of a student's own text looks like this:

> Smiling flower,
> Smiling flower,
> What do you see?
> I see green tree looking at me.
> Green tree,
> Green tree,
> What do you see?
> I see a cute squirrel looking at me.

By producing a text like this, our English language beginners master the frequently used sentence patterns such as "What do you see?" and "I see somebody doing something" and meanwhile expand their English vocabulary.

Using pattern books, students build language sense before they learn grammar rules. They should be able to understand and automatically produce a question like "What do you see?" in speaking and writing before they study the structures of interrogative sentences in the English language. Through creating many kinds of pattern books, our students learn to read, understand, and write simple books and to express their daily life in English.

There are different levels of pattern books, and our students produce their own pattern books according to levels they are reading. Betty started her sixth-grade beginning class with one-sentence pattern books. One example is the book called *Off to Work* by Rom Bacon and Kelvin Hawley. The repetitive pattern in this book is "I put on my (*yellow*) (*hat*) to work." After the class became familiar with this pattern through a practice of speaking and writing with different color adjectives and nouns of clothing (shirt, pants, gloves . . .), Betty introduced them to similar sentence patterns with different verbs, like "I bring my . . . to the school" and "I take my . . . to the park," and some adjectives like *beautiful, lovely,* and *nice* to replace those for colors, and other nouns that fit in the context. The students created their pattern books with all these newly learned patterns and vocabulary to express themselves, such as "I bring my green book bag to the school" and "I take my brother to the park." Betty's students produced two or three pattern books like this a week and practiced reading aloud their own pattern books.

Then, she moved her students to the next level of pattern books, with two- or three-sentence patterns on each page, such as *Jon Sleeps On* by Peter Sloan and Sheryl Sloan. After the students learned the sentence patterns and vocabulary the book introduced, the students used the pattern they learned to

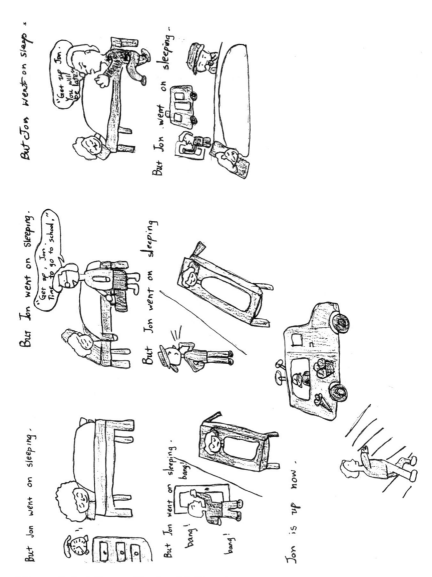

Figure 5–5 A Pattern Book with Drawings

create their own pattern books with drawings (see Figure 5–5). By November, many of the students in Betty's beginning class started to read simple picture storybooks and to write summaries and personal connections as the reading response. But three or four students in her class, who started with ABCs and had little concept of phonetics, even in Chinese, had to stay behind in the pattern books for a much longer time than the rest of the class.

Because students learn at different rates, our teachers often have to move their students to the next level individually. Some students may stay at one level longer than others, and the teachers do not keep anyone at the pattern book stage once they are able to read picture storybooks. John, a seventh-grade ESL teacher, explained that, except for newcomers and one or two students in his class, most of his students in the beginners class grow out of pattern books by Thanksgiving. Because new students come in year-round, pattern books never leave his room and are always part of reading, writing, and oral language activities for the group(s) of newcomers and some struggling students. By December, the writing in John's class starts to diversify in language styles depending upon the reading levels at which individuals are.

Writing with Drawings, Pictures, and Photos

Drawing is a good way for English language beginners to tell their stories. But at first, some of our middle schoolers refused to draw. They thought it was for young children. After much modeling from their teachers, our Chinese students learned to love using drawing to express their ideas. The teachers were amazed by how well their Chinese students could draw, a talent that may result from writing Chinese characters. Chinese is an image-based language, and learning to write each Chinese character is like learning to sketch an image. In our ESL classes and later in their art class, the students drew to retell the stories they read, to express their ideas and feelings in their journals, and to write their own stories (see Figures 5–1, 5–5, and 5–6). Before they could write in English, their drawing was the main text of the stories, with Chinese captions. Gradually, their captions included more and more English words.

Selina, a sixth-grade ESL teacher, used pictures to help her students present their reading comprehension. After the class studied a picture book, she would make copies of the pictures and cut out the text. Then she would ask the students in the writing group to arrange the pictures according to their understanding of the story and write captions for each picture. Originally, she used this strategy to help her students retell the story they learned. After I observed her teaching, I suggested that she let her students say more about each picture, adding their own interpretations of the pictures and enriching the story. In this way, the students not only gave a retelling but also created a new story of their own. Selina was fascinated by the stories her students could tell with the copied pictures. Later, she decided to have the students use the pictures to tell stories before she read a book to them. When she read the story to the class, the students compared their stories with the one read aloud. Sometimes they liked their stories better.

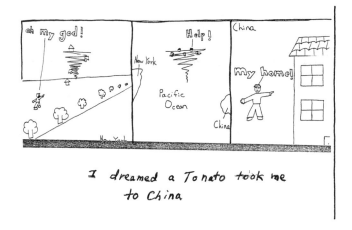

I dreamed a Tonato took me
to China

Figure 5–6 Drawings of Stories

Photos are a big part of our students' lives, past and present. When they tell their stories, they love to share their photos of the grandparents who raised them and of their relatives and friends in China whom they miss every day. They used photos to write their autobiographies and to compare and contrast their lives and their schooling in China and in New York. When they did a theme study on immigrants, they took pictures around Chinatown and wrote about how people lived there. Among their stories, they showed the playgrounds, with many children climbing slides and running around; the restaurants, with roasted ducks hanging upside down in the windows and packed with diners inside; and the apartment buildings, with laundry flying in between. There were also pictures of big trash containers overflowing with garbage on sidewalks and of stores filled with varieties of fresh seafood, meat, and vegetables and crowded with anxious customers. Before they could express themselves with written text, our students used pictures to present their views of Chinatown and their new experiences in America and to tell their stories about their families.

Our students took quite a few field trips every year. They went to museums, to zoos, to Broadway, to uptown Manhattan, and to just see more of New York. Alice purchased disposable cameras with the art project or new immigrant budgets. During field trips, our students would take pictures and notes. Back in class, they would share and talk about their photos and present their learning with individual or group photo books with captions. They could use the language they chose in their caption writing: Chinese, bilingual, or English. With pictures and photos, the monolingual English teachers could figure out what the students tried to say. Drawings, pictures, and photos were, at first, the major texts of our beginning ESL students' writing, when they could write a few words and one-sentence captions. Gradually, when they could write more, especially in English, their written work took more of a front role and their artwork was much reduced in size. Students often preferred their own picture or photo books to commercial ones, because theirs were not only personal but also revealed their creativity and imagination.

Narrative Writing

After Thanksgiving, the teachers started to teach their students narrative writing. The writing topic was usually more controlled and sometimes even assigned by the teachers. In this way, the teachers felt that they could go through the process and work on the language the students needed for their narrative writing. For instance, before Shirley had her students write "My Life" as their narrative piece, she worked with her class for days to fill in the following chart:

	In China	In New York
School		
Home		
Parents' jobs		
Things you like		
Things you dislike		

Then she taught them the language they needed to express their lives: words, phrases, and sentence structures. After the students wrote their first drafts, she taught them how to use transitional words to make their writing cohesive.

Before Betty had her students write their narratives, she let her students write their weekend journals for a month or two, where they wrote in Chinese or mixed languages. From reading their writing, Betty learned what English language she had to teach her students to express their lives. Each week, she introduced them to the English vocabulary and phrases they needed to express their lives, such as "watch TV," "go to the library," "read with my sisters," "do homework in my room," and "play with my friends in the park." After they learned these English phrases, the students had to use them in their weekend journals. After weeks of writing their weekend journals in this way, the students were instructed to choose one of their weekend journals to expand into a narrative piece titled "My Life in America" or "My Life in China."

In their first drafts of the narrative writing, most of the students in Betty's class tended to record moment by moment and end their stories with going to bed. In teaching the students how to revise their work, Betty modeled how to choose a moment or a special incident (zoom-in strategy) to make their writing have a focus and more interest. Going through much revision and editing for three to four weeks, each student in Betty's class contributed a piece to make a story quilt with illustrations on the individual pieces. The following are two pieces out of this story quilt:

Burning Eggs

I felt sad because my eggs turned black. I want to watch T.V. and I didn't watch the eggs. I smelled something awful and the eggs turned black. I didn't know how to cook anything else. But I just know how to cook eggs. I tried to cook again. This time I watched the eggs, and it came out good. It looked as golden as a sun. Now I know I need to watch the eggs and not to go away.

My Story Quilt

I was a baby when my mother went to America. I stayed in China with my grandmother and grandfather. I was very happy because I went with my grandparents to the hills. We sang songs going up the hills. My grandmother said, "I am very happy to have I my husband and Meng Ying going to the hills with me."

I wished next year I can go back to China and go to the hills with my grandmother and grandfather again.

The beautiful story quilt hung on the wall of the classroom and the students were proud of their first class publication.

Helping his students learn to write, John required his students to write a short narrative piece describing their lives every other week starting at the beginning of the school year. They started their writing in Chinese and then progressed to mixed languages (Chinese with English words). Many students began to write their narratives in English after Thanksgiving. A student produced the following piece in John's class after three months in the United States:

My Life New York

I am in New York now. I am I.S. 131 Middle School. There are many different country people in it. They are very funny, so everyday I am happy. Because I have many good friend. They are always play with me.

In my classroom friend a often kidding, So do I were so happy in this school, because we have many good teachers.

I like New York. Because there are many tall buildings, I like my good friend, I hope we can be friend ever!

After Thanksgiving, John instructed his class to read and write biographies. In teaching the students to write them, he first let his students interview each other according to the list he provided: name, birthday, birthplace, appearance, when the person came to the United States, family, hobbies, favorite things, wishes, and a special talent. During their interviews, the students took notes in either Chinese or English. Then they looked for the English words they needed from their Chinese-English dictionaries. After the students worked on their first drafts, they gave the persons they interviewed their writing to read and confirm the information, and they helped smooth each other's writing before they typed it and turned it in to the teacher. John would do some editing, but not word by word, as he stated, "At this point, I want them not to be afraid to write in English, rather than being right."

A struggling student in John's class wrote the following biography:

I am writing a biography on Q. His birthday is on October x, 1990. He was born in Fuzhou, China.

Q. come to America on June 13, 2001. His mother and father with Q. His likes to play computer, watch T.V. and read a book. His favorite subject is ESL.

Q farorite teacher is Ms. Joyce because she can teach student to know a Social Studies. He grow up want to be a doctor. Q wishes is want to fly, have superpowers, and a good brain.

His very special talent is acting.

He has short hair and his favorite color is blue.

Most of the newcomers and struggling students wrote their pieces just like this student, strictly according to the list the teacher provided.

Through their teachers' careful guidance and scaffolding, all the students could produce pretty good writing, including even the most struggling students.

After guiding the students in writing four or five pieces this way, the teachers would give them more freedom in terms of choosing their topics and writing styles. Many students were able to produce readable pieces in English, except a few struggling students, such as the student who produced the piece above.

To work on the writing assignment "My First Time," the student who produced the above piece in John's class struggled for days to think of what to write, then when he finally decided what to write, he took a week to complete it. He typed the following piece on the computer and didn't want anything more to do with it.

My First Time

My first time see look like dog big mouse run for street I and my father was very shocked.

Its teeth are 3 inches long, its tail are 20 inches long, Its 4 legs are 5 inches long. Its eyes are red color and one people run for this mouse. My father walk for this people talk this people and I run to this people listen my father say, "This big mouse one day eat who many food." This people say, "This mouse one day eat 15 pound for food." My father say, "This big mouse 1 hours run who long." This people say, "This mouse 1 hours run 80 miles look like a car the miles." I say, "This mouse live in where." This people say, "This live in dog house." I and my father to this people talk so long.

This people go home. I and my father walk to home, I say, "My first time see this big mouse."

The teacher let this piece be as it was, as he stated: "If he didn't want to work on this piece anymore, I didn't want to push it. To have him just complete a piece is my goal at this point for him, as he struggled so much just to complete a piece in English. If I pushed him to work more on this piece, he might just stop writing. Hopefully by continuing to write piece by piece, he will improve his writing overall."

Reading this work, I realized that this student had a lot to say and it could be an interesting piece. But what he wanted to express was beyond what his English proficiency allowed him to do. In this piece he used specific details to describe a mouse he saw that was "as big as a dog." He used the dialogue to give specific information about the humongous mouse (rat) that he saw for the first time in his life. This piece had a good organizational structure, an introduction and an ending, with a definite focal point. But, it is written in such strong Chinese English, it sounds very broken. I agree with John's decision for students like this one, letting them continue to write piece by piece in English while learning to write and develop their English proficiency will allow them to gradually improve their English writing. (In Chapter 7, I will specifically discuss how to help students improve their writing from Chinese English to conventional English). For the struggling ESL writers, we have to learn to accept their writing in broken English (at the developmental stage), just as we accept their broken English in speaking, with the belief that they will improve their English writing as long as we continue to provide them with writing opportunities, guide them to write, and help them develop English language skills.

Poetry Writing

Poetry writing took place late in the spring for the English language beginners, after they gained much English proficiency to express themselves through reading many pattern books and simple storybooks and creating their pattern books and narrative writing. Most pattern books are written in poetry form and sound like chanting poems with short beats and repetitive rhythm. Through reading and constantly listening to those language patterns, and also writing their own stories, our English language beginners became comfortable writing their own poems.

The difference between creating their own pattern books and writing poetry is that the former is more for language practice and the latter is for self-expression. In short, simple, and repetitive poetry format, our students expressed their personal feelings and views. Susan taught her students to use time lines, five senses, and descriptive words to talk about their memories of their childhood and express their views about their lives in Chinatown and about their old and new homelands.

To write their own poems, they were taught first to choose the topics they cared about the most and then to list the words (nouns, verbs, and adjectives) with which to express their ideas. Later, they were instructed on how to break the lines to create certain rhythmic patterns. With much modeling, Susan's newcomers published their first poems. For example:

My Childhood

I am four years old.
I fall down in the water.
When I get up, I do not see
My mother, I start to cry . . .
I am five years old.
I fall down from the chair . . .
I am six years old.
I fall down from the tree
And break my hand.
Why am I always falling
Down from somewhere?

Chinatown

I'm in Chinatown,
You are in Chinatown
We're in Chinatown!
I see Chinese people.
I touch chopsticks.
I hear Chinese.
I taste tofu.
I smell roasted ducks.
I wonder if this is in America.

China

China
Old, beautiful, big, noisy
Has many parks
Has many different people
USA

These were the poems published in the class anthology, where every student had a page with two or three poems that had gone through many drafts. Susan helped with editing and typing and the students made the cover and the illustrations. The class was proud of their first poetry publication and gave me a copy as a present.

Janet Wong, a well-known Asian American poet, came to our school nine times a year, working with teachers and children in poetry reading and writing. She read the students her poems and shared her thoughts and techniques in poetry writing. She encouraged the students to speak out their emotions and write what they cared about the most in their poetry writing. Janet Wong made a great impact upon our teachers and students, and her writing about her Asian American experience in her simple language and down-to-earth expressions drew great interest among our students. In poetry reading and writing workshops, our students read numerous poems and learned to choose what they cared the most to write about, how to create the rhythm by making each line the same length, and how to stress the meaning by repeating certain lines. Weeks later, they proudly published their first poems in English, as the following:

Seat

I want to change my seat
To talk to girls.
I want to change my seat
To talk to David
About girls.
I want to change my seat

Cause Zhan Zhou bothers me
About girls.
I want to change my seat
To ask Ms. Moulino
About girls.

If You Are in Love

If you are in love,
Your Da and Ma shouldn't know.
You will be very happy.
You will not ask your Da and Ma.
But if your Da and Ma know that,
They will be angry with you.
If I fall in love,
I will do the same.

Sad

I'd like to say
But I can't
Time stops between you and me.
Nothing can stop us.

Wish at Chinese New Year

At Chinese New Year, 2001
I have one wish
To go back
To China
Before Chinese New Year
Is over
I waited,
I prayed,
I prayed,
I waited,
I still can't go back
I don't have my green card yet.

These poems were revised and edited with the help of the teachers, and some even by Janet Wong personally, to be included in the class anthology that every ESL class publishes annually.

After Janet Wong, and their teachers' examples and encouragement, our students learned to openly speak their minds. They realized that their limited English proficiency didn't limit them from using poetry writing to express what lay deep in their hearts. They came to understand that anything they said and wanted to say could be a poem. I was surprised to see how freely these students learned to express their feelings, as if poetry was a path that led them to emotional freedom.

Conclusion

Just like any other students who are developing their writing skills, the beginning ESL students need frequent opportunities to write and need to write to express themselves through many ways and different genres in order to develop their writing competence and language skills. To achieve this goal, we first of all use the students' first language to develop their writing competence in both CLA and ESL classes. In CLA class, the ESL beginning students learn to write essays to present their learning about America. Through the frequent essay writing practiced in CLA class, these students not only continue to develop their writing skills but also learn to present their studies in a new writing format, which is very different from what they learned to write in China. Also, in ESL class, through writing journals in their first language, these students not only are given opportunities to develop their writing skills but also learn to express their reading comprehension and themselves in a way that was unexpected in their formal Chinese schooling (such as personal connection in reading response and writing daily journals).

Second, in both CLA and ESL classes, these students are encouraged to write in mixed languages and choose to write in any language styles in which they feel comfortable. To enable the students to do so, the teachers systematically teach them the English vocabulary and sentences they need. In CLA, the academic English vocabulary is given in accordance with the content they are learning in the American studies; in ESL, the frequently used words, phrases, and sentence patterns are taught daily through pattern books and listening and speaking activities. From reading the students' work written in mixed languages or in Chinese English, our teachers come to know what English skills (vocabulary and sentence patterns) they need to teach to help their students expresses themselves in English. Through encouraging their students to use as much English as possible in their writing and teaching what they need to express themselves, the teachers help them make transitions gradually (without limiting them) from writing in Chinese to writing in English.

Third, the ESL teachers systematically help their students develop their English writing skills. They first use pattern books to develop these students' English reading, writing, and language proficiency. Pattern book writing is practically used for the students to develop their English vocabulary, sense of grammar, and idiomatic expressions. In this kind of writing, the students work on language more than content. After the students master a certain amount of English vocabulary and sentence structures, the teachers guide them to write their narratives and poetry to express their lives. They help them with what to write, what language they need in writing, and later demonstrate how to organize their ideas into cohesive pieces. Gradually they give them more freedom in topic choice and writing styles, and students are required to complete a piece every other week.

Through writing in their first language, writing in mixed languages as a transitional stage, and finally writing in English of different genres, our beginning ESL students are growing as writers and gradually becoming able to express themselves in English. For the ESL beginning writers, allowing individual students to move at their own pace is a must. Among our ESL beginning students, there are always newcomers and struggling students whose first language literacy is three or four years behind their peers. This group of students is moving at a different pace from the rest of the class and needs much more individual attention. Rather than requiring less writing from them, our teachers help and encourage them to write at their current level and often give them more time than their peers to work on their writing. For these students, our teachers show their special sensitivity: when to help, when to push, and when to leave them alone (at their own pace of development as English writers).

For language beginners, speaking, reading, and writing are interwoven. These three skills must develop codependently and reinforce one another. Our students don't wait to write until they've fully developed their reading and speaking skills. As John, an ESL teacher, expressed, we should push everything oral for these students, "to use their writing to speak, to read aloud, to practice using English in public." Our students didn't just write and publish their stories and poems but also read aloud their stories and recited their poetry in class and to the large audience in the library, where teachers, students, administrators, and school staff together celebrated our young authors as writers and poets and, most importantly, as language learners. All their writing, no matter if it is pattern book creation, or captions for pictures or photos, or narrative or poetry writing, should become part of their oral language practice and expression. Their writing is a way for them to express themselves and also prepares them to speak and helps them speak better.

Teaching ESL Writers

Compared with the language beginners, the students I'll discuss in this chapter have much better English proficiency. They are grouped at the intermediate and advanced levels in our school. According to their teachers, the students at the intermediate level can read at the level of second to third grade and are able to express themselves in simple English. Those at the advanced level can read at the level of fourth to fifth grade and are able to speak English quite well. Most of them have been in American schools from two to four years and a few even for six or seven years. In IS 131, the students who haven't passed the LAB (Language Assessment Battery) test are given ESL service and considered ESL students. Without new students coming in frequently, the intermediate and advanced classes are in a much more stable situation compared with that in the beginners classes.

Though I worked mostly with the beginners classes in the last three years, whenever I had a chance, I would take time to visit intermediate and advanced classes, reading through the students' work and chatting with the teachers about their students and their teaching. I was so amazed by the quantity, variety, and quality of writing that our ESL students produced and also by the commitment and excitement that our teachers demonstrated in their teaching of writing. Our school has come a long way in five years.

I remember reading the students' journal writing during my first year of work in IS 131. The teachers had learned to give time and choice for our students to write every day in their journals but didn't know how to help them with their writing. Month by month, the students would write exactly the same thing, recording their daily life thus: get up at 6:30, then put on clothes, eat breakfast, and go to school. I said to the teachers, "If you were bored in reading their work, then they must be so bored in writing it. We have to teach writing. Simply giving time and choice is not enough. We need to help our students learn to express themselves in writing and learn to see more and hear more in their lives." I recommended that the teachers model what they wanted the students to do and show them how they would write in their own journals differently. It took a while before the teachers became comfortable modeling their own writing in front of their students. Now every teacher models his or her writing, though, as Ourania expressed, "It is still hard . . . sometimes."

Students now learn to write in five major genres:

- reading response
- memoirs
- essays
- nonfiction projects
- poetry

Many teachers connected the teaching of these genres thematically. As Ourania stated, she taught memoir, essay, and poetry writing under the theme of immigrants. In this unit, the students learned to use three genres in writing to express themselves, and in the end, they were required to present their work in multigenre styles (Romano 2000). Through learning to write different genres, our students connected their reading with writing, their learning with their lives and their two homelands.

Writing Reading Response

Students were engaged year-round in writing reading response journals in their ESL classes. Teachers used reading responses to check their students' reading comprehension and help them connect the reading with their personal experiences. Different teachers had different expectations of reading journals. Betty liked her students to do double-entry journals in which students recorded the text selection on one side and their responses on the other. Shirley demonstrated four ways to respond: discuss your favorite parts, do a character sketch, make personal connections, and ask questions. She required her students each week to try the different ways of writing she discussed in class. John had his students write pen pal letters to him in which they talked about and recommended the books they read. All the teachers spent time modeling their expectations for reading responses and continuously coached their students individually.

Ourania required her students to read thirty minutes five days a week and write reading responses three times a week. She checked their work once a week and saw reading response journals not only as a way to help her students make reading and writing connections but also a way to build skills as well as to get "their seed ideas from literature for their writing." She started the year helping her students understand the difference between retelling and summarizing and demonstrated how to make connections, as discussed in *Mosaic of Thought* by Keene and Zimmermann (1997). She provided her students with the following four specific strategies:

- Use a graphic organizer to summarize the story.
- Use Venn diagrams to make text-to-text comparisons.
- Use a double entry to make text-to-self connections.
- Use a time line to illustrate the sequence of the story.

When she found that most of her students were most comfortable doing retelling in their reading responses, she pushed them to take risks and try at least one new way each week. In addition, she repeatedly gave minilessons on how to summarize, how to point out the theme of the story, and how to do a craft study of the author's writing. After lessons, she posted on the wall specific examples, such as the following:

Model One

The Wednesday Surprise by Eve Bunting
Summary: Ana and her grandma plan a surprise gift for Ana's dad. The gift is how grandma learns to read.
Message/Theme: It is never too late to learn how to read. Hard work pays off.
Author's Craft:

1. Surprise Ending: In the beginning, we thought it was the little girl learning to read. At the end, we find out it is the grandma.
2. Problem-climax-solution: Grandma can't read. Ana reads with her every Wednesday. Grandma learns to read.

Model Two

The Trip Back Home by Janet Wong
Summary: Janet and her mother went back to Korea to visit their relatives.
Message/Theme: Family—what is the author telling us about the family? She loves her family. Being with the family brings happiness.
Author's Craft:

1. Circular Ending: The story starts and ends in the same setting: beginning, Janet and her mom give gifts and get hugs.
2. Vignettes: Separate events tied together by the same setting.

These models also guided book discussions in class.

Later, wanting her students to be more creative, she modeled how to write a character journal. She shared her own reading response after reading *The Girl Who Hated Books*, which is a story about a girl with a learning disability.

Character Journal from Susan   Oct. 17, 2001

The most wonderful thing happened this afternoon. Tom and I came home from work and found Max curled up in Meena's lap. He looked very cozy sitting there. Meena's face was bright as the morning sun on a cool crispy dry day in fall. And would you believe it, she was smiling and giggling? In her lap, there was a copy of *Peter Rabbit.*

We've surrounded her with books all these years and she's never taken any interest in reading. I don't know what brought on the changes but I like it. I sure hope the magic doesn't wear off.

Many students tried character journals in their reading responses, and one girl wrote her character journal from a different perspective than her teacher did after reading the same book:

My name is Meena. I hate books a lot because in my house books were everywhere. One time, the morning I make basketfast for Max, but he didn't come. You know where he is. He was in a room that had a lot of books. He was on the top of the books. I got safe him, but I splipped down. The character that is in the book were falling out. I want to put them in, but to put them into the book is for them. So I read the books, and they know where they were. Then there were only one rabbit was left. I don't want this rabbit to go back, but the rabbit want to go back so I open the book and let he in. I felt lonely when everyone is gone. Then I start to read. That make me felt better.

Ourania's response was "This was fun to read. Try doing this for other books, too." The student replied: "I will!"

For ESL students, showing models is important. A direction to "make personal connections" may sound strange to our Chinese students, as they were rarely encouraged to do so when they studied in China, where making a personal connection in a book discussion might be interpreted as a digression. Furthermore, they might also wonder how personal they could be in their schoolwork. However, instead of asking the teacher to clarify the direction, they might continue to do silently what they think they should do, such as retelling. Once our students saw Ourania's reading response models, they had fun writing their own.

In addition to minilessons and modeling with her own writing, Ourania also pushed her students individually through her written responses to their journals. In order to understand how she coached her students individually through her written response, I traced their progress in reading response writing from September to December, resulting from Ourania's written feedback.

There were many interesting examples and I will share one of them as a typical example. This is a journal by a boy, an average reader, according to Ourania. In his reading response writing, at first, he only copied from the reading in his journal. Ourania responded: "Please don't copy, but summarize what you read." The student continued to copy. Ourania pushed him again, "Don't copy. Use your own words." After this, the boy only wrote two sentences and seemed confused. Ourania realized that the boy needed more specific direction, so she wrote: "Close your book and write what, when, and where did the story happen? Who are the characters? What do you know about them?" With this specific guidance, the student retold the story with his own words. The teacher was pleased, and she wrote: "This is good and continue to do the same." In the next five pieces, the student used his own words to tell the story, and his retelling became more and more detailed in the later ones. Ourania responded: "You don't have to tell the whole story, just main ideas. Do you have any personal connection to the story or characters? I wonder if you were teased when you first came to the school as Angel girl was in the book." In his next journal, this student made a personal connection:

Title: *Grabby Grew Up*

"I want short hair. Really short, to my ears," Grabby said.

This reminds me of the time I got short hair. Do you think I like short hair like Gabby? No, I hate short hair, I look so ugly when I got hair cut. Every time my parent cut my hair, I'm so sad, even cry. But Gabby looks so beautiful she got haircut. Why am I looks so ugly when I got haircut.

Students not only connected reading with writing but also learned to write their own stories (from making personal connections), to compare the texts (making text-to-text connections), and to read the book with a writer's eye (studying the author's craft). Ourania deliberately trained them to be writers: "From there, I planted the seeds for them to learn to write memoirs and other kinds of writing later."

Memoir Writing

Memoir writing was the most popular writing among our new immigrant students, as they had so much to tell about their lives: the fond memories of their childhood, their unforgettable separation from their homeland, and their shock and adjustment to their new lives in this country. Betty had her sixth-grade students do a story quilt project every year, to which each student contributed a personal story. The quilt hung on the wall of the classroom, and each story was unique and touching. Roza's seventh-grade students did a project on Chinese superstitions. Around the Chinese New Year, Roza's students shared a lot of what they knew about the New Year's taboos, such as "Don't sweep the floor on the New Year's Day or you would sweep away the good fortune that year" and "You can't eat fish on New Year's Eve, or you would lose profit that year." As a class, they decided to do an inquiry project on Chinese superstitions. Each student interviewed his or her parents or relatives about Chinese superstitions and wrote a piece on what he or she discovered:

> In ancient China, when astronomy was still not developed, people didn't know what eclipse was and they never witness one. Until one evening, the yellow moon that hung in the sky suddenly became darker and darker. And gradually, the whole moon was covered with darkness. The witnesses shouted and screamed at the terrible sight. They thought the world was going to an end. But amazingly, after a couple of moments, the moon slowly brightened again and it finally returned to normal. Then the people cheered with joy that their prediction was incorrect. They thought it was the dog who lived in heaven ate the moon. So whenever they see the eclipse, they would walk around their village, stroked their gongs to drive the terrible dog away. After a few minutes of banging and striking, the moon brightened again and the people thought they really drove the dog who lived in heaven away.

From interviewing and writing, our students inquired about their own culture. They came to know why people do certain things during certain times of the year, such as why brides have to wear red, why firecrackers are set out in every house during the Chinese New Year, and why cooked fish should not be touched on New Year's Eve. Most important, this project involved parents and connected with the community.

Our teachers worked hard helping the students with their memoir writing, from getting an idea, to drafting a piece and going through much revision and editing, to publishing and presenting their work. During my visit each month, I was excited to see students' writing hanging in the classrooms and outside the hallways. Whenever I was visiting classrooms, I always read the students' writing from their notebooks, from their portfolios, or from the teachers' desks. In order to gain a complete picture, I observed Ourania, interviewed her, and read her students' portfolios, which contained copies from their notebooks, many drafts, and final products. I collected top, average, and struggling students' work to see how she helped all her students move on in writing. From looking at one teacher and one class closely, I gained a good understanding of how our ESL students with some English proficiency were coached to improve their memoir writing.

Memoir writing was the first genre Ourania tried in her teaching. In the past five years, she has gained much experience in teaching memoir writing, which was part of the unit on immigrants and integrated with reading and reading response journals. To prepare her students to write memoirs, Ourania had the class read stories of immigrants from different countries and make personal connections in their reading responses,

> In this unit, I primarily use picture books to build background knowledge. Students first share what they know about immigration and what they have experienced. All the students in my class are immigrants from China, the Dominican Republic, and Honduras. They share what life in their countries was like and compare it to their new lives in New York. They share their good-byes, airplane rides, and first impressions.

In addition to making personal connections in their reading journals, the students were taught how to do character analysis, to "focus on one of the important characters, and describe what he or she does, says, and looks like." Following is an example from one of the students' works, which was ranked at the average level in Ourania's class:

> *The Tenement Writer* is written by Ben Sonder. This book is about an immigrant from Poland to the U.S. This is about a woman, named Anzia, who was the most hardworking intelligent and outspoken immigrant woman in U.S. history.
>   Anzia worked very hard when she started out selling the herring. She worked in the factory after she sold all the herring. When Anzia saw a girl was next to her apartment, the girl was reading and Anzia went there to ask to teach her English. She pay for the book.
>   Anzia was a very smart girl because she used her mind to think before she does everything. She used 25 cents to buy 25 pieces of herring. She charged two cents for a piece of herring when she sell it all. She had 50 cents and she earned 25 cents.
>   Anzia was outspoken when she was in the factory, she complained to the boss of the factory. The other workers didn't even speak so loud to the boss because they were scared they would lose their work.
>   I understand a lot of things from this book. I know most of them is not like Anzia, outspoken, hardworking and intelligent. Most of the immigrants is working in sweatshops for many more years.

Ourania trained her students to notice details and select the important details to illustrate a character. Before her students worked on their own memoirs, she tried different strategies to train her students to show, not tell, which she thought was one of the key skills.

She had her students work in groups. She gave each group an adjective like *lazy, hardworking*, or *poor* and asked them to collaboratively write one to three paragraphs describing a person who fit the adjective without using the word. Each member was assigned a job: one managed the groupwork, one recorded the writing, one checked the grammar, and one read aloud to the class. Then the students shared the groupwork with the class and let the class guess the characteristics of their description to see if they had described enough to get through their meaning.

Ourania also had her students keep their writer's notebooks and write fifteen minutes every night about their favorite people and events in their lives. After weeks of doing all these kinds of reading and writing in and outside of class, Ourania led her students to work on their own memoirs.

Before they started, the students conducted interviews as a way to learn more about immigrants in real life. They interviewed their parents, family members, or people who immigrated to this country and also each other in class. Ourania worked with them on their interview questions in class and then in groups to make sure they knew how to get people to talk more and tell their stories.

> First, I let them interview each other to learn about each other's lives as well as to practice their interview skills, to tell the differences between "fat" and "skinny" questions. They practiced what good reporters do. For example, how do we get our interviewee to keep talking or how do we change a skinny question into a fat question? They also learned to take notes using their auditory skills for a change.

Before the students turned in their interviews to the teacher, they had to share their findings in groups. The information they obtained from their interviews, their everyday writing in their writer's notebooks, and the text-to-self connections they made in their reading journals all served either as seed ideas for their memoir writing.

I will illustrate Ourania's process by showing how she worked with Tommy, a struggling student, on his memoir writing. She usually spent more time coaching students like Tommy than the others in the class in all parts of the process, from choosing a topic to the final product. Among three drafts Tommy wrote—"Having Pizza," "The Winter Park," and "World Trade Center"—he chose "The Winter Park" to revise and publish. The first draft of his "Winter Park" was written as the following:

The Winter Park

> In 1997 June 17, I went to a park to play, my father, my brother get some picture of me I play Then I went to smiw [swing], I play hide and week I was 10 year old. I and play at the night and I was so happy and than we got to play baseball, I went to play the Pokeman card too.

After conferences with Ourania and peer group response, his third draft became more focused:

The Winter in Park

I am in last winter. I is playing swim [swing] and in night and there have many of snow and I play on monning to night because in monning I play snow ball will [with] my brother in night I play swim [swing] by my salf [self] and I have fun and I think I will play it again but I can't make it because I am big now and I is not small I like to play but I am big and I do not like swim [swing] now. I go to see the swim [swing] many time but the do not have snow. I want to have snow and play.

On this draft, Tommy drew a picture of a boy who was flying high on a swing with snowflakes flying around. Ourania's response to this draft was "Please add more details: what the park looked like, what you saw and did there. Describe everything you see, hear, and smell. Any animals—what do they look like? What are they doing? Any children—what are they doing or look like? How do you feel being there?" After five more drafts and with Ourania's help with editing for grammar and spelling, the final product was born:

The Winter Park

The park has five things. They are swings, slides, baby swings and the last one is the basketball court. I hear kids having fun. I see the kids are happy to play. Then I go to play.

I see some animals in the trees. They are sleeping in the trees. There are many leaves. I see many birds flying in the sky away from here. Maybe they are going to a hot place. Then I find some frogs. I bring the frogs to the ice slides to play. They start to jump and make noise. Then people are catching frogs because they like frogs.

The children are playing in the swings and slides. Some children play on baby swings. I play on the swing, too. Then it is 5:00 pm; everyone goes home but I sit in the park and my father brings dinner to the park. Then we take some pictures. When he takes pictures, I go eat the dinner. The food is rice, fish, meat and some Sprite. The time is 7:00 or 7:30. I start to go home and I remember the frogs, so I go back to bring them home with me.

From the first draft to the final product, there was much coaching and editing involved. Through conferences and workshops, Ourania coached Tommy to write his memoir, and through writing, Tommy developed his writing skills. Though his work was not up to his seventh-grade level and was behind most of his peers, he was growing as a writer while developing his English skills in the context of learning to write about his own life.

Essay Writing

After helping her students write memoirs, Ourania moved her curriculum to essay writing with the same theme of immigrants. She described her goal, planning, and strategies in teaching this part of the unit:

> My overall goal is to examine the patterns of migration, the causes and effects, and the problems and solutions. We are a nation of immigrants, coming from all over the world. In studying this unit, I want the students to go away with an understanding and tolerance for immigrants, other cultures, races, and religions. They understand that immigrants have a tolerance for hard work so that the future generations will have a better life, a life without war, prejudice, and inhumane living conditions.
>
> The students read historical fiction to build their background knowledge, make text-to-text connections, and begin essay writing. I also try to incorporate field trips so that the students can make text-to-world connections. They write cause-and-effect essays after learning about the various reasons why people migrated such as war, famine, natural disasters, lack of freedom, and not just to make more money. With the information they have accumulated, the students write persuasive letters to someone back home convincing them to come or not to come, the way many immigrants of the past did. This is authentic writing. They may choose to send the letters after translating them into their native languages.
>
> Later, students compare and contrast the advantages and disadvantages of life in Chinatown, New York City, versus life in their native countries. In groups, they elaborate on the details of the pros and cons. Then they begin compare-and-contrast essays.

While learning to write different types of essays, the students explored the essential questions for this unit: Who belongs here? Why do people migrate? What problems do immigrants encounter? What are the advantages and disadvantages of migration? What contributions have immigrants made in the United States? Ourania stated, "Throughout the study, we always go back to the essential questions to see whether or not we have gained any new insights to our *burning* questions."

Ourania used the same workshop process approach she used in memoir writing. She coached them to choose a topic, have a focus, add details, restructure the argument, work on the introduction and title, change the wording, and edit grammar and spelling. Without using the five-paragraph essay format to drill her students, she worked with her students first on the main body of an essay. She gave minilessons and walked through the argument with each student, coaching each to give enough reasons to make his or her points and be persuasive enough. After they worked on the body, the students shared their writing in groups to get their peers' response to see if they were convincing the others with their reasoning. After they wrote a strong body, then Ourania gave minilessons on how to start an argument with a come-to-the-point beginning and a summary-like ending. Before reaching final products, she let the students peer edit before she did a final polish for each piece, an editing job all our ESL teachers had to do, as it was impossible for our ESL students to make their work flawless grammatically. Then the students read their essays to the class. Ourania and students worked hard for eight to ten weeks. In the end they were proud of their published work. An example of a persuasive essay produced in class follows:

Dear Xiao Jing Liu:

How are you? My mother told me, you and your family will come to the U.S. I was glad you can come to the U.S., but in Chinatown it is bad. First, the garbage were on the street. The Chinese people did not clean the garbage, and it smell disgusting.

Second, the apartment were expensive and very small room. My apartment is expensive, it cost $800. The apartment has two bedrooms, one living, and one bathroom. My family and my cousin just sleep on a tiny room, the other tiny room someone bought [rented] the room.

Third, if you come to the U.S. you can't see your parents everyday, because your father leave far away from his work. He must wake up very early, so your father must stay there for a week. And you can't see your parents.

Xiao Jing, do you like to see the garbage, to smell disgusting things, to live in a tiny room, and can't see your parents. Do you like your life like that?

Your Friend,
—Wen Liu

Complaining about the living conditions in Chinatown was common among our new immigrant students. Rather than perpetrating their negative feelings about their living environment, Ourania wanted to help her students build more positive attitudes toward their lives. In helping her students write their compare-and-contrast essays, Ourania pushed them to see things from both positive and negative points of view and give suggestions or recommendations for improvement rather than simply complaining.

For practice, the students were paired to interview each other about their views toward a certain issue or a place, and then they each wrote an essay to compare and contrast their thoughts. After going through the same process as they did on their persuasive essay, the students not only learned to write their compare-and-contrast essays but also learned to look at their lives differently. A girl in class wrote:

Chinatown, Good or Bad?

Chinatown is mainly for Chinese immigrants to share their heritage. But, it has its excellent ways and also its defects. Wendy and I compared our ideas about the good and bad aspects about Chinatown to decide whether or not it's a good place for immigrants.

Wendy and I have different opinions about whether or not it's good place for immigrants. She thinks Chinatown is a good place for new immigrants because in Chinatown they don't have to worry about communication problems. They can get used to the lives in Chinatown very quickly, because the people in Chinatown live just like the way they did in China. I disagree with her because if you're in Chinatown you can't learn and speak English very well, because the only kids in school are Chinese. If you speak Chinese all the time, you can't learn English very quickly.

My partner and I both think the lives of immigrants in Chinatown can be improved in many different ways. My partner, Wendy, thinks that immigrant lives can be improved by making streets cleaner, that way the streets won't smell bad. She also thinks their lives can be improved if people can speak softer, that way streets won't be that noisy. For me, I think the lives can be improved if all of them speak English so they can earn more money. This way they won't have to worry about monthly rental payments.

Wendy and I also think Chinatown has some benefits for immigrants. She thinks the parks are places that benefit the immigrants, because they can do exercises there and keep their bodies healthy. I think the library is a benefit for immigrants, because there are Chinese books there and if immigrants read Chinese books very often, they won't forget Chinese that quickly. The library has simple English books so that they can learn English.

I realize that people have different opinions on whether or not Chinatown is a good place. It has benefits for immigrants, but also it can be improved. But for me, I think Chinatown is just fine, and I don't think it needs any changes. I feel comfortable living here because my parents live here but, I miss the trees and clean air of China.

In this essay, the student answered a question that often puzzles people: if, as many of our students complained, Chinatown is dirty, noisy, old, shabby, and expensive, why do the new immigrants who have so little money choose to live there? As this student stated in the end, though she misses "the trees and clean air of China," she feels as if she belongs there because of the familiar culture and people in Chinatown. Chinatown is a place that Chinese immigrants created to shelter themselves from the unfamiliar and often hostile mainstream America. For generations, it has served the same purpose for Chinese and other Asian immigrants, though it has now become an attraction for many tourists. Through learning to write analytically, our students are led to see their community in a positive light and begin to think what they can do to improve their living environment rather than condemning the town that has done so much for the influx of new immigrants for over a century. By writing their views of Chinatown, our new immigrant students learned to think deeper, appreciate their new lives, and see the beauty of their community.

Nonfiction Projects

After reading Stephanie Harvey's *Nonfiction Matters* (1998), quite a few of our ESL teachers became interested in teaching nonfiction reading and writing in connection to thematic studies. In the Countries of the World unit, Betty's sixth graders read books about different countries, did research to find more information about the countries they had a special interest in, and wrote their nonfiction books. Working with the students on their nonfiction writing, Betty demonstrated how to categorize the information they found about the countries and how to structure their writing. After the students completed their first drafts, she worked on other specific writing techniques such as using examples to support statements and having catchy leads and interesting endings.

I happened to observe her teaching a minilesson on leads. She had her students study the opening paragraphs in the nonfiction books they were reading, and then in groups, they discussed the different ways the authors began their introductions. The students grouped their findings into three major types: using a quote, using a question form, and stating an interesting fact. Betty then asked the students to experiment with using these three ways for the introductions for their own writing. "I want them to try to use different techniques in writing leads, though they may decide not to use any one of them for their own piece." Through studying authors' writing techniques and pushing the students to try different techniques in their writing, Betty walked her students through many drafts with revision and editing and helped them produce their nonfiction books with beautiful illustrations. They read aloud and displayed their books to the school audience and also took their books to the neighborhood elementary schools and shared their work with younger children.

Marci, a new ESL seventh-grade teacher, also worked with her students on nonfiction reading and writing in relation to natural studies. During the unit on the rain forest, her students became interested in varieties of animals in the rain forest. They studied different animals and then worked in pairs for their presentations. Each pair chose one animal to study and then published a nonfiction book. Before the students worked on their nonfiction writing, Marci had them study the structure of nonfiction books. As a class, they made a list of the features of nonfiction books and in pairs, they decided what features they would use in their nonfiction books. Marci encouraged the students to try using as many features as possible in their own nonfiction books.

This whole unit took eight weeks to complete, ending with a beautiful nonfiction book published by each pair of the students. Marci was very pleased with the result, "I could have done this unit the whole year, as there is so much we can do and do better." Quite a few students included every feature the class listed from their study of nonfiction books. Their books illustrated their learning not only about the animals they chose to study but also about the nonfiction genre. A book called *Red-Eyed Tree Frogs* amazed me the most. It had a table of contents like this:

- Habitat
- Physical Characteristics
- Food
- Babies
- Glossary
- Bibliography

I will describe a few pages of this book, but my description of these pages can't be even close to the original work, which is filled with colorful artwork, photos, and manipulation of different fonts and layouts in design.

cover page:	Red-Eyed Tree Frog
	[artwork] a big frog with the tongue stuck out by Zheng & Chen
page 1:	Habitat: where red-eyed Tree Frogs are
	Where do we find red-eyed tree frogs?
	We find red-eyed tree frogs in Mexico, Panama, and Central America.
	[artwork] a map of the three places mentioned
page 2:	Where do red-eyed tree frogs live?
	Red-Eyed Tree Frog lived under leaves during the days
	[artwork] a drawing of a tree with a zoomed-in photo attached, in which small frogs are on the leaves
page 3:	Red-eyed tree frogs live in many places like hills, trees and lakes
	[artwork] a drawing of hills and lakes with frogs

page 4:   Physical Characteristics

                   [artwork] a drawing of back part of a frog's body with
                   labels and arrows: skin, back legs, etc.

page 5:   What do red-eyed tree frogs look like?

                   Red-eyed frogs have large eyes on top of their head. They
                   have long and sticky toes, large webs on their feet, strong
                   back legs and bright colors. They have large mouths to
                   eat food. They have large round ears to listen. Red-eyed
                   tree frogs have extra eyelids to cover their eyes. They
                   have bright lime green dorsal and bright orange hands.
                   They are excellent jumpers. They walk slowly. A large
                   frog is 2.5cm/1 inch long from head to tail.

                   [artwork] a drawing of part of the front part of a frog's
                   body with labels and arrows: ear, red eyes, nostril,
                   sticky tongue

page 6:   Why do red-eyed tree frogs have a sticky tongue and
                   sticky toes?

                   [artwork] a photo of a frog and two drawings showing
                   flies on the frog's tongue

back cover: Do you know anything about red-eyed tree frogs? This
                   book is about red-eyed tree frogs. They live in rain-
                   forests. They eat flies. They have big red eyes. . . . Come
                   read and learn more interesting things about red-eyed
                   tree frogs!!! This book is fun!!!

In these eight pages (out of a twenty-five-page book), the authors used
eight of the features of nonfiction books they listed:

- artwork—drawings
- headings
- content description
- photo
- map
- diagrams
- highlighted vocabulary
- synopsis on the back cover

This work demonstrates the students' knowledge of red-eyed tree frogs and
also their understanding of features of nonfiction books. The finished products

reflected the time and effort Marci and her students put into their work and the pride they had for the results of teaching and learning. All these books stayed in the classroom and became classroom resources.

In the past two years, Marci has become passionate about the teaching of nonfiction. Last year, she collaborated with Roza, another seventh-grade ESL teacher, helping students write feature articles and complete a magazine project in connection with a theme study of natural disasters. The students were guided through a process that included drafts and revisions of their writing of feature articles and production of group magazines on natural disasters.

The unit started with reading about different natural disasters. The students worked in groups to create magazines with four different articles about a natural disaster they chose for a focused study. Each group received written directions like this:

> Each article should only be 1–2 pages long, but should have a lot of information. Your magazine should have a front cover and back cover. Each article needs to have: (1) title, (2) at least two or three categories with headings, and (3) three to four nonfiction features. Remember that your magazines and articles need to grab the attention of the readers. They should be colorful, interesting and exciting to look at.

Teachers mapped out the work on a schedule of six to eight weeks, and each day every group made sure they completed their work for that day.

The students composed many notes and drafts throughout this process. A typical folder contained three pages of notes taken after reading two articles about earthquakes. The notes were organized in the following table format.

Source	Topics	Details	Pages
Earthquakes by Anna Claybourne	Earthquake disaster	• An earthquake happens in San Francisco in 1906 • Last for 40 seconds • Very strong • 28,000 building broken • 25,000 lost their homes	page 31

In this folder, there were also six drafts of the students' work about the San Francisco earthquake, two of which were handwritten and four that were typed. Among the six drafts, four were early drafts that were filled with corrections. There also were three different opening paragraphs on separate pages, which revealed the authors' repeated attempts on the lead. After all these revisions, the final product came into being, typed in two columns:

San Francisco Earthquake

On April 18, 1906 at 5:12 in the morning, there was a big earthquake in San Francisco (California). This earthquake was really strong and it moved very fast. The speed of it was 7,000 miles per hour. It measured 7.7–7.9 on the Richter scale.

Damage

First the buildings began to shake and crumble. Then the buildings started to crack and fall down. At 5:13 A.M. the streets began to crack apart. Many towns north of San Francisco were destroyed. Thousands of people died while they were still sleeping.

Effects

As a result of this earthquake, a big fire happened. There were different reasons for this. Some people were cooking and their chimneys were destroyed when the earthquake happened. So fires started. The earthquake also caused the underground gas pipes and wires to break and snap which caused fires in the city. Then the fires got bigger and bigger. The firemen tried to put out the fires, but unfortunately the earthquake also broke the underground water pipes. So the firemen had nowhere to get the water. The earthquake only lasted for 40 seconds but these fires continued for 74 hours. Finally, it started to rain so that saved the town and put out the fire.

Fight for the Future

After the disaster was over, thousands of people left San Francisco. But still many people stayed. This fire and earthquake destroyed about 3,400 acres of land. 28,000 buildings like hospitals, schools and homes were destroyed. 25,000 people lost their homes and all of their belongings. All the homeless set up camps in parks. Some also built shacks. Many people from other states sent out water, food, and medical supplies to San Francisco. Some people also lent money so the people could rebuild buildings after the disaster was over. The people had positive attitudes and began to rebuild the buildings so they were stronger. Within a year San Francisco was crowded again.

One interesting fact about the San Francisco earthquake was the scientists discovered that animals did weird things before it happened. Dogs howled throughout the city and horses jumped around nervously. So seismologist think that maybe there are some sound waves from earthquakes that only can be heard by animals.

This was one of America's worse natural disasters. There were four major earthquakes that happened in San Francisco between 1979 and 1989, but this one was the worse one ever.

After students finalized their feature article writing, the group designed a magazine layout and illustrated each page as well as the front and back covers. On the day of my visits, the students were working in groups, designing the layout of their group magazines. They used many commercial magazines as models to create their own.

I was impressed with what our students had learned about nonfiction. Though not every student was able to produce the same quality as the piece shown here, they all learned how to search for and organize information and also what it took to produce quality work. Furthermore, they were learning academic language in the context of reading and writing about the world.

Poetry Writing

I remember the first year when Maureen introduced poetry to ESL classrooms, some teachers resisted. "Poetry is just not my thing. If I have to teach it, I will do it, but I can't write poetry." Now, poetry is taught in almost every ESL classroom, and every student can proudly call himself or herself a poet. They write poems on many subjects, but mostly to express their feelings and thoughts. Every year in almost every ESL classroom, there are class publications of poetry anthologies, many of which include the teachers' poems. In the acknowledgments of the first poetry anthology published by Mae's eighth-grade students, they wrote:

> The students of classes 817 and 818 were unsure of how to write poetry until Ms. Janet S. Wong came in and demonstrated to them the techniques she used. During this time the students themselves read and worked on many poems—writing, editing, and revising. While many changes can still be done on these poems by professionals, it is an excellent first attempt at writing poetry by English as Second Language students.

Since their first attempt at poetry writing, Mae and her students couldn't stop writing poetry throughout the year. It seemed there was a poetry fever everywhere in our school. Janet Wong, an Asian American poet, contributed a great deal to this happening in IS 131. During her visit to the school, she gave Saturday workshops on poetry writing to the faculty and worked with teachers and students in classrooms on poetry reading and writing. In between her visits, our teachers and students would send her their poems for her to respond to. She gave each individual detailed feedback for revision, editing, and encouragement. All students and teachers in IS 131 formed a special bond with Janet Wong, through either reading her poems or working with her individually on their own poetry writing.

I recalled the first time I attended a poetry reading by the ESL students in the library. Present were all the school administrators, ESL teachers, resource room teachers, and paraprofessionals as well as every ESL class. Also among us was Janet Wong. Class by class, the students read aloud their poems to the big audience. We applauded after each reading, feeling both touched and inspired. Ourania joined her seventh-grade class and read the first poem she wrote, which began:

My Father

My father
Was a lonely man
Who talked to his comrades
in his tiny Brooklyn apartment.

Ourania was the first teacher who shared her own deeply personal writing with the school audience. She cried while reading her poem. Girls wiped their tears and boys held back with a solemn, stony silence. Her poem tied us together at that moment.

For four years, Ourania taught poetry reading and writing in connection to her thematic unit on immigrants. Her students produced numerous poems each year. When I asked her to share with me how she made this happen, she showed me a packet she compiled in the spring of 2002, which included many ideas she learned at Janet Wong's workshops. In this packet, she explained in detail her instruction in poetry teaching. She attached her students' work to each minilesson she taught—it could have been a textbook for poetry teaching. Here I can only present briefly some strategies she used. I hope some day she will write her own book on teaching ESL students to write.

1. Warm-Up for Poetry Writing

While teaching students to write memoirs and essays in this unit, Ourania incorporated poetry reading every day for a few minutes on the topics related to immigrant experiences. When poetry became the focus, her students had gained appreciation for it. At the first stage of poetry writing, Ourania tried different strategies as warm-up exercises. She first had her students write poems by imitating others. It was very much like how we had the English beginners create pattern books: she used simple poems with a repetitive style to guide her students to write their own poems. After she modeled how she imitated a poem she liked to create a similar one, her students began to try their own. They paralleled their own poems with the poems they imitated:

Noodles	**Hamburgers**
Noodles for breakfast,	Hamburgers for breakfast,
Noodles for lunch,	Hamburgers for lunch,
Noodles for dinner,	Hamburgers for dinner,

Noodles that crunch,
Noodles to twirl,
Noodles to slurp—
I could eat noodles
All day! Burp!

—Janet Wong

Hamburgers that sizzle,
Hamburgers that drip,
Hamburgers to devour
I could eat hamburgers
All day! Burp!

—Huang

My Grandmother

My grandmother
  is a honey colored woman
  warm as the sand
  on her tropical island.
My grandmother
  is a tall straight woman
  swaying like the palms
  on her tropical island.
My grandmother
  is a talking woman
  chattering like the green parrots
  on her topical island
My grandmother
  sweet sugar woman
  I love her so.

—Lori Marie Calson

My Grandmother

My grandmother
  is a gold colored woman
  strong as the iron
    in her town.
My grandmother
  is a tall skinny woman
  soft as the paper
    in her town.
My grandmother
  is a quiet woman
  quiet like an ant
    in her town.
My grandmother
  Sweet friendly woman
  I love her so much.

—Qiao Qing Zheng

After her students created their poems by imitating many kinds like this, Ourania used templates as guides for the students to create their own poems. For example:

Line 1—Name an emotion or feeling and finish the line with a color word.

Line 2—Tell what it sounds like.

Line 3—Tell what it smells like.

Line 4—Tell what it tastes like.

Line 5—Tell what it looks like.

Line 6—Tell what it feels like.

To follow this template, the students wrote their poems like this:

Sadness

Sadness is gray
It sounds like the moan
of a foghorn.
It smells like mushrooms.
It tastes like stale popcorn.
It looks like a lost puppy
Sadness feels like damp clothes.

Another strategy she tried was to let her students play with the English language in poetry writing by making a list of adjectives or verbs that described a person, a place, or an object, then revealing what they described at the end. Her students wrote:

Jumping	Crunching	Cooking
Running	Munchy	Cleaning
Laughing	Oily	Washing
Crying	Salty	Working
Skating	Crispy	Yelling
Rolling	Potato Chips!	Mother! Mother!
Eating	Potato Chips!	
Playing		
Growing		
Kids! Kids! Kids		

After two or three weeks of writing poems by imitating others, according to different kinds of templates, and under certain guidelines, Ourania's students learned to play with the English language and poetic forms. These were like warm-up exercises to loosen them up for real work.

2. From Prose to Poetry

Ourania believed that if the students could write good narratives, they would have a good base for poetry writing. She asked them to start writing a prose piece with the following directions:

- Tell me something or someone that is special to you.

- You can also write about ordinary things or events.

- Write a paragraph about this person, thing, or event.

- Describe this person, thing, or event with details.

With experience in memoir writing, it was not hard for her students to produce a piece as expected. Here is a typical example:

Today is 12-10, 00. The weather is cloudy and sunny. I was riding on the train, I saw a man hold a bag and say: lady and gentleman, part of me, I live on the street. I don't have a home, please help me.

After he say the words, he took out a cup and walk around the train, but no one gave money to him, I want to give him so money, but I can't if give him, I don't have enough buy things.

I think the man is very poor, because now is winter, and he don't have enough clothes to keep him warm, and a house to live, things to eat, when I saw this man, he made me remember Clay. Clay is a homeless who don't have a house and no cash money. I wish I have more money, if I have more money, I will gave so to him.

After the students wrote their prose, Ourania taught them how to break lines, or transform a prose piece into a poem. The student changed the above narrative into a poetic form:

I am riding on "N" train
I see a homeless man
He says,
Ladies and Gentleman
Pardon me
I live on the street
I don't have a home
please help me.

After he says the words
He takes out his cup
Walks around the train
No one gives money to him
I'd like to give him some
But
I can't

Another student tried two different ways to change her prose into a poem:

Draft 1

My grandmother, short and thin.
Wakes me up on the morning
Runs in the kitchen and fixes
Breakfast, combs and braids
Her black hair. Long and
Beautiful strands that shine
In the sun. Runs off to work
With her hair flying in the sky.

Draft 2

My grandmother,
Short and thin
Wakes me up
In the morning
Then runs in the kitchen
and fixes
breakfast
while I eat
she combs and braids
her black hair
long and beautiful strands
that shine in the sun

when she runs off to work
with her hair
flying in the sky.

Ourania taught her students to break the lines according to meaning, to rhythm, and to a feeling they wanted to convey to the readers. After they learned how to do this, their confidence in poetry writing soared up and they couldn't wait to try more. But Ourania continued to teach them to do better and be more creative in poetry writing through her numerous minilessons.

3. Minilessons for Revision

Ourania presented numerous minilessons she taught to help her students revise their poetry writing. The first one was to use repetition of a line in every stanza, which is like a refrain in music. After she modeled the technique, her students produced poems like this:

My Little Brother

My little brother
throws garbage
around the house
so I pick it up for him.

My little brother
doesn't clean
the house
so I clean it up for him.

My little brother
hits me everyday
and I let him hit—

Before I tickle him back, OR
while I laugh, OR
something else to show us
what a good person you are!

In another minilesson, Ourania taught the students to play with voices and verb tense in poetry writing. She showed them first to use narrative voice: "It is like newspaper reporting. It's in the third person. Present the story as it happened. Take out the "I." Just tell the facts." She shared an example:

Sue

When Sue was little
her mom
dressed her in pretty
pink dresses
washed her face and hands

Sue
walked down the steps
out the door
SPLASH
into the spraying water
CRASH!

Then she demonstrated how to change that same poem into a lyrical voice. Ourania explained this by saying, "The poet puts herself in her poem. Use *I, my.*"

When my sister was little
my mom
dressed her in pretty
pink dresses . . .

She also had her students play with the tense, such as writing a poem with present and past tenses to experience the distant and close effects the verb tenses give the reader:

When I was five
Some summer evenings
Mom took us
To the nearby park to play.

I am five
On summer evenings
Mom takes us
To the nearby park to play.

After teaching the students to play with verb tense, she taught a minilesson about using the "voice of mask." In this voice, the writer pretends to be someone or something else in the poem. Ourania showed them many poems written from a voice of an animal, a tree, or a snowflake. One student tried a poem from the voice of a slave child after she studied the Civil War in her Chinese language arts class.

Slavery
The sky is dark,
I use my tears
to wash my face.
I will never see
my mom again.
I am lonely,
I will miss a lot of
happy times with my mom.

But why did she auction me?
Does she care

that I'm leaving here?
I am sad,
I am a child,
Who doesn't have
a mother's love,
And a family's love.

The class had fun writing poems with the "voice of conversation" after Ourania showed them Janet Wong's poems written in this form. A boy in the class wrote this poem:

Jobs

What kind of job do you have?
> *A cook in a restaurant*
> *How about you?*

The president of the U.S.A.
> *You must do a pretty good job.*

I think so.
Do the customers like the food you cook?
> *Yes!*

How much money do you earn a year?
> *About twenty-four thousand dollars*
> *How about you?*

I earn two million.
> *That's a lot of money.*

I think so.

In addition, Ourania also coached them to try the techniques of personification, or "giving human-like qualities to objects." She helped them play with shape of a poem, "creating a picture of an object by writing words related to that object." Rather than constricting her students with certain strict poetic forms, Ourania taught them different ways to write their poems, to play with the language and forms, and also to develop a joy in expressing themselves in poetic forms.

Through teaching with minilessons, modeling with her own writing, and conferencing with individual students, Ourania gradually cultivated in her students confidence and competence in poetry writing. They wrote poems to express their sweet and sad memories for their hometowns, their lost childhood, and the relatives they left behind:

Whenever I Comb My Hair

Whenever I comb my hair
I look in the mirror
And I feel my grandma's hand
Helping me comb my hair

When I look in the mirror again
I am so sorrowful
The hands I see are mine.

Fishing

Fishing with your friends
The big green forest is at the back
Fish swim around in the river
Cows eat grass
Bird fly around the sky
What a wonderful countryside
I used to live!

They wrote poems to question their future:

Future

Future, future
Where are you?
I am looking for you very hard.
Jason, Jason,
I am here
Waiting for you to come
Future, future
where are you?
I am getting confused about you.
Sometimes I think you are next to me
Sometimes I feel you are far away from me.

They wrote poems to question their social standing:

Piano

I see rich children
Every day they stride
And hurry to class
For piano
Lessons.
They hit the keys
With lovely
Sound coming
Out.
I hope I'll have
A day like
That.
Da Di Di Da
It's my lovely sound.
It's the first sound I can
Play on the piano

Even in my dream.
I hope I can have piano
Lessons.
I wonder when?

They wrote poems to define or search for their identity:

Everyone wishes for something
Jewelry,
Money,
Being pretty.
But they are different from me.
What I want is a genius brain,
Good grades,
And good health.
Different people have different luck.
My name gives me luck
Smart luck,
Gives me intelligence to figure
Right and wrong.
That is my luck.

They also wrote poems to understand poetry:

What is poetry? I know.
It is music,
Can be sung in different ways
It is picture, in the mind.
It is waves,
Moving up and down.
It is a rainbow,
Full of color.
It is a mystery,
You need to discover.

Nikoleta's students not only wrote and compiled their poetry anthology every year but also reflected upon their learning of poetry reading and writing. Here are some excerpts of their reflections on their learning experience:

> Before when . . . people asked me what is a poem, I didn't even know. Now when I write poems, there needs to be strong words or adjectives. . . . I know how to write a good poem.
>
> —Ye Ying

> When I wrote my first poem, it made me want to write more. . . . My favorite poet is Langston Hughes. Most of his poems are about African Americans, and I want to write a poem just like him, but I will write about Chinese people.
>
> —Jing Peng

Poetry is amazing and interesting. When I read the poems, it made me have different feelings, happy, sad, funny, excited. Like Annabel Lee, by Edgar Allen Poe, it made me feel so sad. I can learn a lot of things in poetry.

—Zhuo Qi

There are different ways to write poems; dramatic voices and conversation. . . . It feels so interesting and exciting. It's fun learning poetry.

—Xiao Lan

Every semester in my college-level language arts methods course, I do a survey of the preservice teachers' attitudes toward poetry writing. Among thirty students in a class, there are always less than 10 percent who claim that they love poetry writing. Most of them think it is something incomprehensible in reading and intangible in writing. Fortunately, the teachers in IS 131 have made poetry part of our students' new literacy and new lives in this country.

Teaching Writing to ESL Students

While writing this chapter, I constantly asked: Is there a difference between teaching writing to native English-speaking students and ESL students? Our ESL teachers described in this chapter used the same strategies and approaches in teaching their ESL students to write as those discussed in the books of Harwayne (2001), Rief (1991), Atwell (1998), Harvey (1998), Calkins (1995), and Graves (1995), which are used by teachers as resources or guides in teaching writing all over the country. In general, there is much similarity in teaching writing to native English-speaking students and ESL students; to help students to think, to develop their thinking and to organize their thoughts, and then to present their ideas in Standard English. Maureen Barbieri's book *Change My Life Forever* (2002) has powerfully demonstrated this point, showing how she helped Chinatown new immigrant students write. The ESL teachers in IS 131 successfully adopted the strategies and approaches advocated by researchers like Graves and Calkins and promoted by exemplary practitioners like Harwayne, Rief, Harvey, and Atwell in teaching their ESL students to write. The general progress that our ESL students made in their writing and language abilities and the overall joy they demonstrated as writers and language learners proves that the approaches that work for native English-speaking students can also work for ESL students.

But our ESL teachers may have to do more in some aspects. They need to give more specific directions and modeling of their expectations. They spent much time and effort not just helping students revise and edit their work but also helping them understand what they were expected to do. The teachers also spent more time on language conventions than teachers do with native

English-speaking students. In my observations, I noticed the teachers constantly remind their students of tense, plural forms, and gender or language inflections and help the students pay special attention to their diction and use of idiomatic expressions in their reading and writing. But the teachers knew how important it was to recognize when to do more and when to do less. This is a delicate balance for our ESL teachers. In the drafting stage, they usually ignored the language conventions and focused on the content and ideas in their students' writing, just as they did with their students' broken English in their speaking, though they occasionally grabbed a teachable moment to reinforce the English language rules the students had learned but often neglected. For instance, a student would say or write *I am* in the first sentence, and in the second sentence, she would say or write *I is.* In this situation, the teacher would pause and ask "I is?" or underline *is* to remind the student of the language error. As Ourania explained, when the students make these kinds of errors, usually they know the concepts but haven't formed a habit. It is a careless error rather than a conceptual one. Knowing how to help students form good language habits without interrupting the flow of their thinking and speaking is a key skill for all of our ESL teachers.

During the editing stage, our teachers spent a lot time and effort working with language skills in writing through minilessons, peer editing, and individual conferences. Before the students presented or polished their final products, the teachers worked with students individually on grammar, spelling, word choice, and idiomatic expressions. In reading, they instructed the students to notice diction, and in writing, they coached their students to use different idiomatic expressions such as "come on" and "traffic jam." On the walls in each room were posted vocabulary words related to a certain theme or descriptions of a certain mood or action. In teaching writing, our ESL teachers paid special attention to the development of their ESL students' language skills and vocabulary development.

In addition, our ESL teachers paid great attention to connecting their students' writing with their oral language development. Their writing, after being revised and edited many times, became the refined version of their thoughts and emotions. Therefore, when their writing became the base for their speech, their oral language became more polished and sophisticated. Our teachers tried to help their ESL students speak out everything they wrote. Before they shared and presented their work, their teachers would help them polish their grammar and spelling. In order to avoid rewriting for the students, the teachers often had to keep the Chinese-English expressions in their students' work, which was a special voice at this stage in their writing.

To help the ESL students improve their speaking ability, our teachers required the students to share their reading journals and memoir stories, to present their nonfiction projects, and to read aloud or recite their poetry. The students practiced reading their work at home and in groups and rehearsed with the teachers before they presented to the class. Very often, the teachers had to spend almost an equal amount of time and effort in helping the students with revision, editing, and preparing for presentation. Through speaking out their writing, they became better English speakers and writers, as Ourania stated: "I really feel that the more a student talks and reads, the more fluent his or her writing becomes," and vice versa.

In IS 131, our teachers don't let our new immigrant students wait to write until they develop their reading and speaking skills in English. Instead, they help them develop reading, writing, listening, and speaking skills simultaneously. In writing, the teachers teach the new immigrant students as well as provide them with time and choice to express their emotions and thoughts while helping them develop their English language skills. They coach them continuously to grow as writers, readers, and speakers.

7

Language Differences and Errors

All ESL students' speech and writing are unavoidably influenced by their first language when they begin to learn English. The later a person starts to learn a second language, the heavier or more persistent the influence of his first language. Very often, English language beginners at the middle school level appear to have more language errors in their English speaking and writing than those at the primary school level because they started to learn English at a later age than the primary grade children. They also must cope with the more sophisticated topics and ideas in the middle school curriculum.

Chinese and English are very different languages. When our new Chinese immigrant students first write in English, their writing marks typical Chinese English—English words written in Chinese syntax. The Chinese English can appear so strange that it overwhelms our non-Chinese-speaking ESL teachers. At a workshop, many ESL teachers complained about their Chinese students' writing: "We don't know how to begin to correct their grammar. Their sentences are out of place, no subject, no verb, and it is like a bunch of words randomly grouped together." I knew exactly what caused their frustration. Chinese has a totally different structure than English, and when two languages mash into a language like Chinese English, it can appear or sound like gibberish. Here comes a dilemma: When teachers are overwhelmed with the surface structure, it is hard for them to get into the meaning without being troubled or even offended by the "errors." But when we pay too much attention to the students' language errors, especially at the drafting stage of their writing, we may tend to focus our instruction on the language, but not on writing or writers. If we did this, our ESL students would be pressed to learn *how to be right* rather than *how to write* in English. As Shaughnessy (1977) stated, "So absolute is the importance of error in the minds of many writers that 'good writing' to them means 'correct writing,' nothing more" (8).

130

In order not to paralyze our ESL students or magnify their inadequacies by pointing out their seemingly random or illogical errors, we ESL teachers need to understand the causes of those frequently made "errors" in our ESL students' speaking and writing. With that knowledge, we won't feel their errors are that offensively incomprehensible or annoying. During the five years of my work in IS 131, I gave several workshops about the Chinese language and its differences from English, which usually were the roots of the common errors the Chinese students made. In this chapter, I will share what I presented at those workshops and discuss how we should look at our students' errors and help them develop Standard English.

The Chinese Language System and the Tradition of Language Learning in China

The Chinese language is an ideographic language and English is a phonetic language. In Chinese, there is little relationship between how a word sounds and how it is spelled (looks). Every character is an image, or several combined imagery parts formed together as one character. A word in English may be several characters in Chinese, such as the word *school*, which is formed by two characters, *study* and *campus*, in Chinese. For example, our Chinese students would write *Chinese* or *Chinese people* as *China people* or *a China man* using their understanding of how a word is formed in Chinese to construct English words and phrases. Chinese characters and words are conceptually constructed. When Chinese children learn to read and write Chinese characters or words, they have to learn the relationship between their shape (or their structure) and their meaning. It differs fundamentally from the English language, whose spelling corresponds with how it sounds rather than what it means.

Though learning Chinese characters requires forceful memorization, there are some patterns to follow, such as certain symbols associated with *hand* and *water*. The characters like *pull*, *push*, and *pick* associated with *hand* would have the symbol of *hand* as part of the characters, and the characters like *lake*, *sea*, and *ocean* would have the symbol of *water* as part of the characters.

The rules for handwriting in Chinese are very strict because a slight difference in a stroke (e.g., if it is too long or short) or a dot missing in a character can make it look like a different character. Penmanship has been a tradition in the Chinese culture for centuries and all schoolchildren have to practice writing characters legibly every day from the first week of their schooling until they master the skill. The conceptual structure of the Chinese language (characters and words) makes it impossible to separate the practice of handwriting from learning the meaning of the characters or words.

In modern Chinese, a phonetic system (pinyin) has been created to help people learn to pronounce Chinese characters. The twenty-six letters used as the Chinese phonics are the alphabetical letters in English (based on Latin) but sound different than English phonics in certain vowels and consonants. Schoolchildren in China have to learn this phonetic system in order to pronounce Chinese characters. They are trained to use two methods of learning the Chinese language: phonetics to pronounce the characters and graphic memory (sight-word strategy) to remember the construction of characters or words. Because all Chinese students are trained to use these two ways in learning the language at school, I found that most Chinese ESL students don't have much problem with spelling English words, compared with other English language skills in their learning. Also, Chinese ESL students tend to have quite a good handle on handwriting in their English writing as a result of their hard practice of penmanship in the Chinese schools. Yet, wide differences between Chinese and English interfere with the learning of English, especially English grammar.

The Differences Between Chinese and English Grammar

The physical appearance of the Chinese language makes it look difficult to learn, but its grammar is quite simple when compared with many inflectional languages (including English). Let's look at the verb first. The Chinese language doesn't have verb tenses. Rather than changing the verb tense, it uses adverbial words or phrases such as *yesterday, tomorrow*, and *at this moment* to indicate the time—past, future, or present. The contrast between English and Chinese is as follows:

In English	*In Chinese*
I went to work.	Yesterday I go to work.
I am going to work soon.	Soon I go to work.
I am working.	I right now work.
I have done my work.	I finish my work *or* I already do my work.

In the Chinese language, verbs don't change with the subject, either. The contrast between the Chinese and English is as follows:

In English	*In Chinese*
I am a teacher.	I *is* a teacher.
She/he is a teacher.	She/he *is* a teacher.
We/they/you are teachers.	We/they/you *is* teacher.
She has a child.	She *have* a child.
Susan studies English.	Susan *study* English.

Therefore, there is no such concept as inflectional verb endings in the Chinese language—causing a huge difficulty when the Chinese learn English.

Also, there is no distinction between transitive or intransitive verbs. In this sense, all verbs can be followed by a noun as an object, such as *I read a book*, and *I go the store*. Therefore, the use of a preposition between a verb and a noun, such as *go* to *school* and *deal* with *a problem*, can be a new concept to the Chinese ESL students. And the concept of the infinitive *to* between two verbs doesn't exist in the Chinese language. The contrast between the two languages is as follows:

In English	*In Chinese*
I want to see a movie.	I want see a movie.
I went to the store to play a game.	I go store play a game.

Nouns in the Chinese language remain the same regardless of number. Chinese uses a number or a quantity adjective to indicate more than one, such as *two book*, *many child*, and *a few egg*. Nouns are always spelled the same, as there is no capital form for any nouns in Chinese. There is also no difference between countable and noncountable nouns, like *books* and *water* or *air* in English. Therefore, we can say *many book* and also *many water* or *many air* in Chinese.

In the Chinese language, pronouns don't show the difference between subjective and objective cases: *they* and *them*, *he* and *him*, *she* and *her*, *I* and *me*, and *we* and *us*. For example:

In English	*In Chinese*
I told him to come here, but he didn't hear me.	I tell he come here, but he not hear I.

In colloquial Chinese, sometimes the pronouns (*I* and *she*) and possessive adjectives (*my* and *her*) can be used to mean the same thing, such as *I father* used interchangeably with *my father*. And there is no difference in possessive pronouns and adjectives, such as between *mine* and *my* and *theirs* and *their*, in the Chinese language. Because of all these differences between the Chinese and English languages, the typical grammatical errors in the Chinese ESL students' writing (and speaking) are

- verb tense
- inflectional endings
- the use of the infinitive *to*
- subject and verb agreement
- plural forms and their verb agreement
- the use of subjective, objective, and possessive pronouns and adjectives

Though these errors appear annoying or confusing to listeners and readers, they usually don't affect the central meanings that the speakers and writers try to convey. Once the students learn the rules, it is a matter of forming habit through practice. They need to read, speak, and write often and have self-correcting and editing practice to eventually gain a good command of these English language skills.

The Differences Between the
Chinese and English Sentence Structures

The syntactic differences between Chinese and English present the greatest difficulty for the Chinese ESL students in making their Chinese English sound weird and incomprehensible (see the example of a student's narrative writing in Chapter 5, page 94). The simple sentence structure in Chinese and English is very similar: subject + verb + object, such as *My friend read a book.* Chinese says it in the same sentence order. The difference appears in the two language structures when one adds an adverb, or an adverbial phrase, or any modifier for the subject, the verb, and the object in a sentence. For instance, the English sentence *Yesterday my friend read a book in the library* has the following sentence structure:

adverb (Adv) + subject (S) + Verb (V) + Object (O) + Adverbial phrase (Adv-p)

Yesterday   my friend   read   a book   in the library.
  (Adv)   (S)   (V)   (O)   (Adv-p)

To express the same meaning, the Chinese would be *My friend yesterday in the library read a book.* Its sentence structure is

My friend   yesterday in the library   read   a book.
   (S)   (Adv)   (Adv-p)   (V)   (O)

The rule in English is that the core structure of a sentence (S + V + O) should stand closely together, and the other parts should go before or after the core sentence. But in Chinese, a modifier mostly goes before the word it modifies. Because *yesterday* and *in the library* in the above sentence modify the verb *read* (when and where to read), they go before it in Chinese. This Chinese-English sentence order breaks the basic rule in the English syntax, so it sounds awkward to English speakers.

This difference in sentence structure between Chinese and English becomes wider when a sentence grows more complex:

Yesterday   my friend   whom you met before   read   a book   recommended
                                                                by her teacher

  (Adv)   (S)   (Adj-c = adjectival clause) (V)   (O)   (Adj-c)

for two hours   in the library   before she went home for dinner.
   (Adv-p)   (Adv-p)   (Adv-c = adverbial clause)

In this English sentence structure, the core sentence structure (S + V + O) stands not too far apart, and the modifier clause goes after the noun it modifies. In Chinese, the same meaning would be expressed as:

Before you meet that   my friend   yesterday before she go home for dinner
(Adj-c) *as modifier of*   (S)   (Adv)   (Adv-c)

in the library   for two   hours   read
(Adv-p) *three Adv(s) as modifiers of*   (Adv-p) (Adj-c) *as the* (V)
recommended by she teacher that book.
modifier (O)

The difference between the Chinese and English syntax is the Chinese breaks the so-called core structure (S + V + O) with the modifiers in between, which always go before what they are associated with, no matter if they are words, phrases, or sentences (clauses). This difference in sentence structure causes errors in the Chinese ESL students' writing. A sentence like the one cited above would make no sense to any English readers. They would not know where to begin to figure out its meaning. That is why direct translation or word-for-word translation from Chinese to English or vice versa never works. When we see the differences between two languages, we understand that when one learns a new language, she does not only have to learn different vocabulary and grammar but also has to reconstruct her thinking order and adjust to new language patterns. David Olson (1994) states, "Our graphic systems not only preserve information but also provide models which allow us to see our language, our world and our minds in a new way" (258). When we speak a different language, we may think differently too. I have heard that some Westerners complain that Chinese people don't seem to speak straightforwardly but take a long time to get to the point. The different order of the Chinese language structure may contribute to this impression.

Other differences in sentence structure between the Chinese and English languages include the following:

- A Chinese sentence can omit a linking verb, like the verb *to be* in English. For instance, in Chinese we can say: "My father not at home, he at school."

- Sometimes a Chinese sentence uses double verbs together, such as "I is work hard." The verb *is*, which functions more like *do* in English, here stresses *work*.

- A Chinese sentence can omit a subject, such as "Tomorrow have no homework."

- The subject can be omitted in a subordinate clause in Chinese. For instance, to express the English meaning "I think I will go to the store to play video games after school," the Chinese would say, "I think today after school go game store play video game."

- The *it* that indicates time, weather, and temperature in English, such as "It is Friday," "It is cloudy," and "It is hot," doesn't exist in the Chinese language. We have to say "Today Friday," "Today cloudy," and "Today hot." We often see expressions in Chinese ESL students' writing like "It today Friday," as they don't know what *it* stands for in this sentence.

- Chinese only has one word for the meanings of "to have" (to possess) and "there is/are" (to exist). For instance, we would use "to have" in the following two sentences: "I have many books" and "My apartment has many books."

- A "because" clause is followed by a "so" plus a sentence in Chinese. For instance: "Because he is sick, so he can't come to the meeting."

- A "though" clause is followed by a "but" plus a sentence in Chinese, such as "Though he was very sick, but he came to the meeting."

- The subclause with *if, when, because, after,* or *before* has to go before the main sentence; for example, "When she came, we had finished our work." It is not in the right order in Chinese if the sentence reads: "We had finished our work when (or after) she came."

There are numerous differences between Chinese and English grammar. Here I only discussed the ones that are the causes of the common errors that our Chinese students tend to make. Because of these differences in sentence structure between the Chinese and English languages, the Chinese English that our English language beginners tend to write can appear weird, incomprehensible, and overwhelming. Here is a typical example of a beginner's work:

> Today, I 8 o'clock get up. I go to the school, I in the school eat the breakfast. In the CLA the class the Ms L give we are Wednesday test back. I just 51%. I think is very not good. I think today after the school go to the game store play the video games. Tomorrow I will go to the school study the ESL. And I and Wersua go to the shopping buy the some thing. I go home eat the dinner and watch the TV watch the video and many thing, I feel tomorrow is very happy.

This piece reflects first language interference and is a typical piece written in Chinese English. This paragraph consists of mostly simple sentences. While awkward, it is still readable. If this piece were written with more complex sentences, it could have sounded much more awkward and incomprehensible.

The differences in sentence structures also create great difficulty in reading formal writing, especially that written in an academic style. It is not just the vocabulary or terminology but also the complicated sentence structures of the English language, such as sentences (subordinate clauses) within a sentence (a main clause), that are hard for Chinese ESL students. When I taught English in China, the complex sentence structure of the English language was the most challenging topic for students.

Other Differences Between the Languages and the Errors They Cause

The differences in expressions and word usages in the two languages are also roots of the language errors in the ESL students' English learning and make them sound awkward to English speakers. One of the common and most persistent errors among all Chinese ESL students is the use of the article *the*. In the Chinese language there is no such article. For the same purpose as *the* is used in English, the Chinese use *this* or *that* and *these* or *those*. Since the use of the article *the* can sometimes be so arbitrary or simply idiomatic in English, it is extremely difficult for Chinese ESL students to know how to use it correctly, especially for those who learn English in their later years (after twelve or thirteen years old) or who don't have opportunity to thoroughly immerse themselves in the English language environment in their daily lives. I have learned English for almost thirty years, and I still have problems in using the article *the* correctly.

The next most common error among the Chinese ESL students is the use of prepositions. Since much preposition usage in English is simply idiomatic, it is difficult for new- or latecomers to have a good grasp of it. When I learned English in China, I was taught to forcefully memorize the use of prepositions as verb or noun phrases, such as *deal with, search for, arrive at* and *at home, in a factory*, and *under the condition of*. I found that this kind of unit memorization was more helpful than memorizing prepositions in isolation but wished I were provided with more reading and writing opportunities to go along with the memory drills. After years of English learning and paying special attention to language when I write, I still frequently make errors in preposition diction in my writing. Since I always have someone clean my work before I send it out, this handicap usually doesn't affect my meaning and doesn't hurt me much as a writer, but it does frustrate me as a language learner. A preposition looks so small and even so insignificant in a sentence, but it can be so hard to get it right.

Gender pronouns are another source of frustration. Even though in writing, the Chinese language has different pronouns for gender difference, like *she* and *he*, all three pronouns (*she, he*, and *it*) sound the same in Chinese speaking (*ta*). That is why when the Chinese ESL students speak English, they often mix *he* and *she*, while they can do a better job when they write. I still make this mistake in my English speaking though that rarely happens in my English writing. This stubborn erroneous habit in my speaking often embarrasses me greatly, as it can really confuse listeners.

The other common errors our Chinese ESL students, especially the beginners, tend to make in their English speaking and writing are verb usages. In Chinese, we use the same verb for *read, look, see*, and *watch*. I found that the new ESL students often wrote "I see a book" to mean "I read a book" and "I look TV" to mean "I watched TV." They made the same kind of mistakes as they failed to tell the differences among the words *take, bring, get*, and *fetch*, between the verbs *live* and *stay*, and among the words *any, some, much* and *many*. The reason for making this kind of error is that in Chinese, either there is only one word for the meanings that English slightly distinguishes, such as *take* and *bring*, or the words can be used interchangeably in Chinese, like *read* and *see*.

In the Chinese language there is often no distinction between adverbs and adjectives. For instance, we use the same word, *beautiful*, in these two sentences: "She had a beautiful voice" and "She sang very beautiful." And Chinese has only one word (*hao*) for *good* and *well*. All these features in the Chinese language interfere with the English learning of our Chinese students. Although the wrong usage of these words and expressions can be quite annoying and confusing in our ESL students' writing and speaking, it usually diminishes quite quickly. After a few months to a year of intensive English language learning, our ESL students made fewer mistakes of this kind.

In addition to the differences in grammar and word usages, there is an obvious difference in semantics between the two languages, which can cause a confusion or even a misunderstanding. In English, for the question "Is he not coming?" usually the answer is yes if the listener thinks he is coming or no if he thinks he is not coming. But to a Chinese speaker, the answer would be just the opposite, because the answer yes means "Yes, I agree with you that he is not coming." If the answer is no, that means "I don't agree with you and he is coming." It took me quite a long time to get it right. And even today, once in a while, I still confuse people with my yes or no responses to certain questions. I think an explanation of the difference in question response between the two languages would be a great help to our students.

Pronunciation

According to Noam Chomsky (1990), if people start to learn a new language after seven or eight years old, it is impossible for them to speak the new language without any accent. Though I don't believe the absolute age cutoff he asserted, I agree that most ESL students will have a certain accent in their English speaking if they start to learn English in their teens or later or if they don't have an opportunity to be immersed in an English-speaking environment, like the children in Chinatown.

I remember at a conference after Ken Goodman gave a talk about language learning, a teacher from the audience asked a question: "How can we help our ESL students get rid of their accent?" Goodman's response was "Why should you get rid of their accent? I think accent is beautiful. We all speak with an accent. It would be so boring if we all spoke the same" (1994). I felt so good and empowered by Goodman's words. He made me proud of my accent for the first time in my life.

I remember when learning English in China, we had to use a mirror to see where we should place our tongues to pronounce English words like *think* and *sheet* and put two fingers into our mouths to pronounce the word *bad* and one finger into our mouths to pronounce the word *bed*. We worked so hard to get the pronunciation right. When I came to America, I realized that what we did was too much, as few people here really distinguished their pronunciation of *bad* and *bed* that much. And after I worked that hard in pronunciation practice, my accent remains anyway.

I think that we need to help our ESL students with their pronunciation, not to get rid of their accent completely but to help them speak English properly and comprehensibly. Because of the numerous differences between Chinese and English, there are certain sounds that are especially hard for the Chinese students to pronounce, such as /r/, /l/, /sh/, and /th/. Generally, /r/ and /l/ consonant sounds don't exist in the middle and at the end of a Chinese character, and /sh/ and /th/ sounds don't exist in Chinese. The Chinese students who start to learn English have to first learn to hear (receive) these sounds before they can learn to pronounce them. It takes a lot of practice for them to readjust their tongues and mouth muscles to get the right pronunciation.

There are hundreds of dialects in China, and the speakers with the various dialects encounter different challenges in English pronunciation. Students who can speak several Chinese dialects usually learn to pronounce English sounds with much ease. This means their sound-receiving ability is much stronger and their tongues and mouth muscles are much more flexible. Of our Fujianese immigrant students, most can speak two dialects: Fujianese (the local one) and Mandarin (the standard one). The few who can only speak Fujianese have many more problems in English pronunciation than those who can speak more dialects in Chinese.

The biggest challenge for the Chinese students in learning English pronunciation is the syllabic stress and weakened sounds in a word because the Chinese language is a monosyllabic language. Each character has one syllable and most characters end with a vowel, such as *ta* (she, he, or it), *wo* (I), and *ma* (mother), except ones that end with /n/ (*lin*) and /g/ (*zhang*). A character may have different tones with different meanings. For example, *ma* with different tones can be mother, pox (like chicken pox), horse, and scold. Homophones are one of the main features of the Chinese language. Some characters may each have several dozen homophones, such as the character *si*, which has more than ninety homophones. In different contexts with different tones, *si* carries different meanings.

An English word with several syllables, such as the word *characteristic*, is a new way of reading to the Chinese. In pronouncing the word *characteristic*, some Chinese may put the stress on the last syllable and also add the /er/ sound at the end of the word. This wrong syllabic stress and slight addition in word pronunciation can make their English-speaking sound very strange and incomprehensible. In English, the past tense of a verb with the inflection *-ed* ending and the preposition *to* always has a weakened sound, like *worked, liked, waited to see, talked to the teacher*. Our English language beginners have to practice very hard in learning to pronounce the *-ed* sound close to their throat and the *to* sound behind their upper teeth, trying not to make them visible in pronunciation. In a similar way, sound clusters like *ask, lift, world*, and *act* and consonant blending like /gl/, /gr/, /bl/, /br/, /sp/, and /st/ in English are very challenging for new Chinese ESL students to pronounce because there are no such consonant blending sounds in the Chinese language.

There is not any shortcut to get pronunciation right. That is why we had our English language beginners listen to pattern books on tapes and also practice reading every night as homework. It is a painstaking effort and time-consuming work. This kind of practice requires students to work on their own or in pairs and at their own pace. For our middle school–aged students, it can be an embarrassing practice. It is better for them to practice reading at home or privately before they are asked to do it in public.

Reading Students' Errors and
Helping Them with Their Language Skills

It is hard to read ESL students' writing, especially the language beginners' writing, without being drowned or overwhelmed by the errors that are everywhere on a page. When we understand the root of the errors, which is the students' first language interference, we know that our ESL students don't make those errors randomly in their writing but write consciously or unconsciously according to the underlying patterns of their mother tongue.

When ESL students learn to speak and write in English, they have to break the code they have learned since their birth and reconstruct their thinking patterns and reregister their language orders. Learning a new language is learning new concepts and forming new habits. When we read the ESL students' errors in English writing, we need to look at them developmentally. That is, to see what they have learned but haven't gotten right. It is like when a child says, "I goed to the park yesterday"; developmentally, this child has learned the concept of the past tense, but she has overgeneralized the rule for past tense. This child has made an intelligent error. In this case, we should celebrate what this child has learned and that she is able to apply the rule she has learned in a new situation before we try to help her say it right.

To help teachers look at the students' writing from a developmental perspective, I asked our ESL teachers to look for the skills that the students had learned as language learners when reading their writing. For practice, let's read the following piece, a journal written by one of our Chinese new immigrant students who came to this country only four months before he wrote this piece.

> yesterday Ms. M go to take the book and give we see. The book title is Martin Luther King Day. In 3:00 O'clock, I and my friend go to Broadway shopping and 7:00 O'clock go home do the home work and see the book and go to sleep. Today I 6:30 O'clock get up the bad and go to brush my teeth and wach my face and eat the breakfast.

Let's first list the English language skills this student demonstrated in this piece:

- Capitalization: He started all new sentences except the first one with a capital letter and also capitalized the special nouns and the book title, like *Ms. M*, *Broadway*, and *Martin Luther King Day*.
- The use of infinitive *to*: e.g., *go to take, go to sleep*, and *go to brush my teeth*
- The difference in expressions between *go to Broadway* and *go home*
- Compound sentence: *Ms. M go to take the book and give we see.*
- The English expressions of *brush my teeth* and *wash my face*; in Chinese, we never use *my* in these expressions
- Good spelling skills

In four months, this student learned a lot about the English language. He learned all these new concepts, which don't exist in the Chinese language.

After we discover what this student knows about the English language, we form a positive perspective about this student and his writing. Next we move to help the student improve his writing. As language teachers, we all understand that we shouldn't correct every error in our ESL students' writing. Then what is the next step to help this student with his English language skills?

It appears that the big problem in his writing is tense. But I don't think this student is ready to work on the past tense. He hasn't used any past tense in this piece, which means he hasn't learned the concept about verb tenses in the English language yet. He would be confused or overwhelmed if we helped him correct the tense in every sentence in this piece. I would leave the tense problem alone at this point but help him correct a few errors such as changing *see the book* to *read the book, in 3:00 o'clock* to *at 3:00 o'clock*, and *give we see* to *give us to read*, and moving *at 6:00 o'clock* before the subject instead between the subject and the verb. These changes would smooth the piece greatly and would also be manageable for the student.

Our students' errors often inform us what we should teach. This piece has shown that there needs to be instruction on past tense. Since learning the verb tenses involves learning about new sets of verbs, only the teacher knows when his students are ready to handle this task. If I were the teacher, after I taught the past tense, I would have my students revisit some writing they did before and make corrections on tense usage themselves.

When our ESL students tried to write more and express more complicated ideas, they made more errors. Here is a piece written by a student ranked at the intermediate level:

> My house has a hall and a room. My hall have a TV is square, have table and chair, have settee and carpet, have bed is balk and read, have a pendant lamp and paintings, have a telephone.
>
> My room have a bed is rectangle, have a TV and wardrobe, have window curtains, have a telephone, and wall calendar, have a sofa and vase, have a yellow desk. My house yet have a toilet and a kitchen.
>
> In my house, I heard my sisters said that one teacher in my school has tear one of student's ear. When his parents know that, they went to school, and yell the teacher. And, that teacher has to pay the money and quit her work.
>
> America is second country I been. The first time I am not ready like this country. I feel scared, and no freedom.

I can tell that this student tried to describe his house (apartment) in detail and then told one thing that happened at home. He concluded the piece with what he thought of America. The teacher sent me this first draft and asked me to discuss the language skills and errors displayed in this piece in a workshop I conducted on language. I trusted that the teacher would work with the students on the content revision and I simply focused my attention on the language.

Reading this piece, I found that this student had attempted to compose in complex sentence structure and wrote a few structures correctly, such as "I heard my sisters said that . . . ," and "When his parents know that, they went to. . . ." He was taking risks to write sentences with relative clauses like "My hall have a TV is square [which is square]," ". . . have a bed is balk and read [which is black and red]," and "America is the second country I been [I have been or lived]." Though he didn't write them correctly, he knew that a relative clause should follow the noun as a modifier, which differs completely in Chinese. He began to experiment with the past tense and also the present perfect tense ("One teacher in my school has tear one of student's ear").

This student has also begun to understand one of the key features of the English grammar (tense shift) and the complex sentence structures of the English language (a main clause with a subordinate clause). I think this writer is ready to learn the difference between *to have* and *there is/are*: "There are a TV, a bed, and a desk in my apartment." He needs to pay attention to the use of past tense, when to use *has* and *have* and plural forms in order to gain a good command of these skills. Regarding the complex sentence structure. I think we can show him the right way but not make a big deal of it at this point. He should have more language experiences with reading and listening to complex sentence structures and gain a sense of them before he is given a formal lesson on grammar, such as sentence diagrams. Anyhow, this student is already at the initial stage in learning to write complex sentences in English.

It is interesting to note that the word *yet* was used as *also* in the writing. I found that most of our Chinese ESL students relied heavily on their electronic dictionaries, which gave them English translations to the Chinese words they inserted. Frequently, for one Chinese character, a few English words with similar meaning would appear, such as *yet* and *also* and *like, love, affection,* and *passion*. Students often randomly choose one and have no idea of the different meanings of these words. That is why we often found that our ESL students used some big words, like *intrepidity* to describe a tiger and *introversion* to talk about a friend, and some words in a wrong context, like *yet* used in the piece cited above. Making errors in word choice is a natural stage for all ESL writers when they don't have a big vocabulary pool and have to compose in English. After maturing as language learners and writers, they will have less tendency to make mistakes like this.

Suggestions for Teaching
English Pronunciation and Grammar

This chapter entirely focuses on language structure and skills. I deliberately structured this focus as a late chapter of the book, as I wanted to convey my belief in ESL teaching that teaching content and thinking should be the center of any language instruction. In order for our students to develop their language skills, they have to be immersed in content-rich and personally meaningful language experiences. Maureen Barbieri has demonstrated this point very well through her book *"Change My Life Forever"* (2002). They should develop all the language skills, which are listening, speaking, reading, writing, and thinking, at the same time.

In the previous chapters, I have discussed in detail how the ESL/bilingual teachers in IS 131 helped their new immigrant students develop their listening, speaking, reading, and writing skills in the context of their study of the content knowledge. In the initial stage for the beginners, the focus in the ESL class was more on the language development than on the content knowledge, which was mainly covered in the CLA class. For the first three months, the goal of the ESL instruction for the newly arrived students was to help them develop the English language skills that would enable them to function in the classroom and the school and in their daily lives. Gradually their study of content knowledge became heavier. According to John, a seventh-grade ESL teacher, the goal for beginners in the seventh grade was to help the students develop from zero to second-grade English proficiency within a year—an ambitious task. By the end of the year, 75 percent of the students reached this goal the team set, though the students' speaking and writing had obvious traces of their first language interference. In the following sections, I will share suggestions for helping our new immigrant students lessen their mother tongue's interference with a focus on the instruction of specific language skills. But I sincerely hope this will not lead the ESL teaching away from the real reading and writing. Isolated instruction on language skills should not become the core ESL curriculum.

Helping the Students with Their Pronunciation

Listening and speaking should go together. The students (of middle school or above) should practice reading and speaking on their own with pattern books. Teachers need to read aloud and do shared reading with them in small groups daily. Because Chinese students tend to have problems with the rhythm of the English language and blending sounds, and lack the sense of syllable stress and weakened sounds in a word, we should pay special attention to these aspects. For listening, reading, and speaking practice, I suggest the following strategies:

- Train the students not to read word by word, but to read a phrase as a whole. For instance, let them practice reading "go to school," "in the library," or "by myself" as a whole unit without a pause between the words.

- When reading language units as cited in the previous suggestion, they should learn to stress the key words, such as *school, library*, and *myself* and weaken the others.

- Students should listen, pause, and imitate when listening to books on tape. They should underline the words or phrases they have difficulty with and ask their peers or the teacher for help.

- As teachers, we should identify students' individual pronunciation problems and give them specific help. For instance, many Chinese students have problems with the /r/, /l/, /th/, /sh/, /ch/, and /v/ sounds. And a majority of the newcomers have difficulty with syllable stress when pronouncing multisyllablic words, like *difference, problem*, and *characteristic*.

- Have students read aloud every day (at home and buddy reading in class) and train them to gain reading fluency with the right pauses and rhythm in a sentence in order to achieve fluency in reading and speaking.

- Once the students gain reading fluency, encourage them to speak a phrase or a sentence without reading word for word.

- Require them to speak up in class. Let them prepare what they will say before they are required to speak in class. Speaking broken English is better than speaking nothing at all.

- As John promoted, make everything oral in ESL teaching.

- Engage students in reader's theater, puppet shows, plays, songs, and music.

With so much practice in listening, reading aloud, and speaking, the ESL students will gain a sense of the English language, not just in pronunciation but also in grammar and sentence structure. If they can make themselves understood better, they will be willing to speak up and feel comfortable communicating with English speakers.

Helping the Students with Their Common Grammar Errors

Reading provides opportunities for ESL students to encounter the Standard English language structure. Writing gives them chances to experiment (hands-on) with the English language. It is like learning to swim. The learners need to see how others swim and also need to jump into the water to feel the water and learn to kick and breathe. ESL students need to constantly read and write in order to master the English language skills.

We should teach the English grammar tenses gradually, but it doesn't mean we should let the students read only the texts written in the present tense before they are taught the past tense. One of the ESL teachers in IS 131 was afraid that her beginning class would get confused with the grammar tenses, so she rewrote every book she had her students read into a text with only present tense before she taught them the past tense. Not only was it a very time-consuming job for her, but also the rewritten texts became very boring.

It is okay for the students to encounter a new language phenomenon before they learn it. Usually, a reader tries to understand the meaning of a text and ignore the features of the language at the first reading. Only after she figures out what it means will she pay attention to certain language features. Also, it is good for new language learners to read the real language and encounter many different language features before they study them. It is like children learning to talk. Though we do simplify our language when we speak to babies, we rarely use only one-syllable words and only present tense in our speech. According to Heath's study (1983), the Roadville community residents speak to their babies just the same as they speak to anybody else. Their children all grow up to become competent speakers of the language they have been immersed in since their birth. When ESL students formally learn a new language skill, they should have had some experience with it (through listening or reading) for a while. It is good if they raise questions about a grammar skill phenomenon. When they begin to ask questions about certain skills, they are taking the initial step in learning the new concepts.

I recommend we teach the present tense, past tense, and future tense at the same time when we are ready to talk about grammar tenses. Because students have already had the concept of time difference, what is new to them is the different way to present this difference. The ESL students of middle school age or higher understand the concept of tense shift. But to form a habit and use those tenses correctly requires effort and practice. In many years of my teaching, I found that when the students made errors on their grammar tense, it usually was not that they didn't understand the concept, but that they were not used to the new rules. New ESL students haven't established the English language habit. So when they speak and write in English, their words flow out of them following the pattern of either their first language or the English grammar with which they are the most familiar (which is often the present tense). When the students study three or even four tenses (including present continuous tense) together, they can compare and contrast the differences in tense usage by seeing them side by side.

Another difficulty for Chinese ESL students is the use of prepositions in idiomatic expressions, such as *at home*, but *in the library* and *to be familiar with* and *to get rid of*. It is hard to explain why certain prepositions are used in certain places but not in the others. This is the arbitrary feature of a language. One of the effective ways to learn English prepositions is to memorize a prepositional phrase as a unit rather than remembering individual prepositions in isolation.

Reinforcing the learned skills is the key in language teaching. Students have to constantly hear, read, and use those skills in meaningful contexts. I have seen the ESL teachers in IS 131 constantly remind their students of the English rules such as subjective and objective (or predicate) agreement, verb tense usages, plural forms, and the usage of subjective and objective pronouns. To enforce the language skills, I suggest these strategies:

- Every student should have a checklist of grammar rules he has learned.
- Students self-edit their homework according to the checklist before they come to the class.
- Then have students peer edit their work in class before they turn it in.
- Give minilessons on the common errors in your students' work.
- Then have a conference with a pair of students (who edited each other's work) at a time to discuss the errors that remain in their work.
- Have students write down what language skills they should pay special attention to in their writing after the meeting.
- Have students periodically evaluate their own improvement in their language learning and set goals for what skills they should work on next.

This is time-consuming work, but there is no shortcut or easy way out. To form a language habit is a lifelong task. We have to help our students as much as we can when they are in school, or they will feel handicapped when they leave us to join the mainstream society.

Helping the Chinese ESL Students Learn English Sentence Structure

When I was writing this chapter, I had to look more closely at my mother tongue with an analytical eye and I realized some features of the Chinese language that I had never thought about after using it for my whole life. When I realized the differences between the two languages, I wished I could have done some language comparison study with my students when I taught them English years ago in China. I remember the frustration they as the students and I as the instructor went through in learning and teaching those complex sentence structures and trying to understand and explain a sentence order packed with several relative and adverbial clauses.

I think a language comparison study would benefit the ESL students of middle school age or higher. I don't recommend we should do this sentence study with the younger students, as providing rich language experiences should be the main strategy for them. But I also don't recommend that for the older students we should diagram a sentence to death or teach the grammar in isolation. That can be very destructive and makes language learning very distasteful and boring. We should do this language study at the editing stage or even only with a small group of students when they are ready for it. In a language comparison-and-contrast activity, we can have two sentences stand side by side, of which one is written in Standard English and the other in

Chinese English (using our students' work). Then we can explain or contrast the logic behind the language structures of the two languages. In doing so, we will let the students see what is "wrong" in the Chinese-English sentence and help them transform their writing to Standard English. Showing the differences in sentence structure between their first language and English is like giving our ESL students a map they urgently need when they have to move across the territory of the languages.

Of course it is hard for non-Chinese-speaking ESL teachers to do a comparison study between the Chinese and English languages. Hopefully this chapter will help the non-Chinese-speaking ESL teachers gain some understanding of their students' Chinese-English writing and be able to make sense of their "weird" errors. In teaching the Chinese students the English sentence structure, I suggest that we need to explain to them the essential elements and the core structure of an English sentence. That is:

- There is always a subject and a verb in a sentence.
- The core structure is S + V (He walks) and S + V + O (He reads a book).
- The adverbial words and phrases should go before or after the core sentence, such as "Yesterday I read a book in the library."
- The clause functions as a modifier and always follows the nouns to which it relates.

To the Chinese students who are just beginning to learn English, these are brand-new concepts. From learning these basic English language structures after they have had some English experiences (listening and reading), they will gain a good conceptual understanding of the English language and compose fewer awkward Chinese-English sentences in their writing.

Showing the ESL students how an English sentence grows (expands) can also be an effective way to teach the English sentence structure. For example, we can show how to expand a sentence in the following way:

> *I read a book.*
>
> Yesterday *I read a book* in the library.
>
> Yesterday after school *I read the book* in the library.
>
> Yesterday after school *I read the book* recommended by my English teacher in the library.

After this demonstration, we can have our students pick up a sentence from their own writing to do this sentence expansion exercise. In connection to their reading activity, they can pick a long sentence in the book they are reading to find the core sentence (S + V + O) and see how the other parts are related to this main body. This exercise may sound boring to others, but to new language learners (not young primary students), it is kind of fun because they are tackling a brand-new structure and need to make some sense out of it.

I want to again emphasize that ESL students need plenty of listening, speaking, reading, and writing activities in meaningful contexts. Very often, ESL instruction focuses more on language skills than content in reading or thinking development in writing. Even when it is integrated with a subject area, the emphasis is still on the language skills. We do need to teach grammar and other language skills, but we need to think about how we teach, and when to teach more or less of certain language skills. Making mistakes is not only unavoidable but even necessary for all ESL students in their language learning. The more risks they take in English speaking and writing, the more mistakes they will make. We need to make sense of the errors they make and look at them from a developmental perspective. We should let those errors inform us of what we should teach and how we can help our students improve their language skills.

Conclusion—Issues and More Questions

School as a Learning Community

In the past five years, under the leadership of Alice Young, the faculty, administrators, and all the school staff in IS 131 have worked hard to improve the instruction and search for the most effective ways to teach new immigrant students. Now this school has truly become a learning community. The CLA teachers continue to improve their instruction through collaboration with the ESL and social studies faculty to make their students' learning more connected. The ESL teachers constantly add quality literature to their class libraries, working to make reading and writing more interesting and meaningful to their students. From reading the students' personal reading responses and writing, the teachers are gaining a deep understanding of their students as individuals, their lives, and their families. This understanding continues to help the teachers form a nurturing relationship with their students and also to inform them about what they should teach and how they should approach their students.

Now in IS 131, every teacher sees her- or himself as an ESL teacher. English listening and speaking activities are seen not just as part of ESL teachers' work but as part of every instructor's, and in every subject our ESL students are learning. Our students practice English speaking and listening in art, music, and dance just as much as they do in ESL classes through writing their scripts, presenting their work, and performing their shows. The students in IS 131 are not quiet learners anymore, and teachers no longer work only in their own territory.

All the hard work has paid off. According to the New York City Department of Education's statistics (2002) at its website *www.nycenet.edu,* IS 131 was among the top 10 percent (24 out of 220) of middle schools in New York City that ranked "Far Above Average" in their effectiveness, based on reading test data. Among the twenty-four schools ranked "Far Above Average," IS 131 was the only one whose student population consisted of a majority of "most needy" students classified as Category 8 (from the least needy as Category 1 to the most needy as Category 8).

It is a law of physics that, once an object is set in motion, the movement will continue, and in the same direction. That is happening in IS 131 under Alice's leadership. The school will continue to make changes for the benefit of its students, as it has been doing in the past five years. My work in IS 131 has finished and what I have learned there has enriched me as a teacher educator. I am carrying what I have learned from the teachers and students there to other Chinatown schools, where I continue to grow through meeting new challenges and solving new problems. My work in IS 131 has also deepened my thought in the area of ESL, bilingual, and literacy education, the literacy education and standard for new immigrant students, and many other ethnic and cultural issues. In the following sections, I will present my discussion on these issues.

Bilingual Education, English Immersion, and Literacy Education

In this book, I discussed how bilingual education, ESL education, or English immersion developed for a very challenging student population. As a matter of fact, I don't know how I should define our ESL/bilingual program in IS 131. In the Chinese language arts program, which is defined more as a bilingual program, our teachers employ both Chinese and English in teaching, and the students read and write in both Chinese and English or either one as their choice. In the ESL program, which is defined more as English immersion, the students, mostly in our beginners classes, also read and write in both Chinese and English, and gradually they do so solely in English. In these two programs, the teachers can claim they are both bilingual and ESL teachers, as there is not a clean-cut distinction. Instead of confining themselves to the definition of bilingual education or English immersion, our teachers use any possible way to help the new immigrant students develop their American literacy and English language skills.

I am very frustrated with the polarized debate in recent years on the education for students with limited English proficiency—bilingual education (to use the student's primary language) versus English immersion (to use English only). Our work with new immigrant students in IS 131 demonstrates that either one can work effectively for students with limited English proficiency. These students need to use their primary language to learn the content knowledge and continue to develop their literacy skills as readers and writers before they gain enough English proficiency. Because of the nonideal English language environment at home and in the community where these students reside, ESL/bilingual teachers in IS 131 have to maximize English exposure at school for their students. Therefore, they have to make their Chinese language arts program more ESL than bilingual, according to how ESL (English immersion) and bilingual education (using the students' primary language) are often defined in the country. As a matter of fact, the CLA program in IS 131 well deserves to be called bilingual, as both the teachers and students are using Chinese and English (bilingual).

Those who oppose bilingual education think that bilingual education prevents the ESL students from spending the time and effort they need on English learning and blame bilingual education for the low academic performance of ESL students. They believe that by totally immersing the ESL students in *English language–only* situations, they will be thoroughly soaked in English so they will be transformed into English speakers and writers within a year or two. But the cause for low academic performance of ESL students is much more complicated than simply not spending enough time studying English, as I explained through the examples of the Chinatown new immigrant students in Chapter 1. I made simple suggestions, too, on how to speed up English language learning for these students when I first worked in IS 131. I tried to suppress the students' first language and encourage English only in school for our immigrant students, but that suggestion didn't work and I was forced to adjust my thinking. A well-known saying is "A simple answer to a complicated question is doomed to be wrong."

Supporters of bilingual education believe that it is important to use the students' primary language to build content knowledge and boost self-esteem for the students' mother tongue and home culture. Our work in IS 131 has proved this to be right, though we have done more. For the benefit of our Chinatown immigrant students, we include English literacy in our bilingual education and give the students a choice of the language they read and write in, in order to let them fully display their competence and explore their potential as literate persons. For the needs of their school learning and life transition, we teach them about America instead of China in the bilingual program. It is important to maintain our students' home language and culture, but we believe that an ignorance of their adopted homeland would not only make them always feel like outsiders in this society but also give them a false understanding of America, which many believe is only a place to make money and get rich. To teach about America is to help them see the beauty of this nation, understand the essential reasons for people to immigrate to this country, and prepare for their transition into becoming Chinese Americans. We see the study of America as being more important and necessary than simply maintaining their home language and culture.

In the field of literacy education, we clearly define the line among bilingual, ESL (English immersion), and literacy education. Bilingual education is to use the students' primary language for instruction, English immersion is to use *English only* to develop the language skills, and literacy education is for reading, writing, and language arts instruction. In IS 131, we integrate them all. And our integration has greatly benefited our new immigrant students. Through our integration of bilingual, ESL, and literacy education (and content area as well), the students are developing their competence as readers, writers, and English language learners (both of social and academic language) at the same time.

Interestingly, because of the clearly defined lines of these three areas, I am accepted as a researcher only in literacy education in our professional world, not as one in bilingual or ESL education, even though my research on the ESL/bilingual students is well read and adopted by many ESL and bilingual programs in the country. In my job searches in the past, I realized that I was driven out the door of the ESL and bilingual education programs. I even received a call once from a university, nicely telling me that they were impressed with my vitae but didn't think I was trained enough in the ESL and bilingual fields, so they were sending my application to the literacy program for consideration. When I sent my manuscripts on research of ESL students to *TESOL* or other ESL journals, they turned me down, saying that I sounded like too much of a literacy researcher rather than an ESL or bilingual person. I lack their discourse. But in Chinatown schools, I am often referred to as "the ESL lady."

In the current professional world, in both natural and social sciences, there is a deafening call for interdisciplinary collaboration. As education researchers, we are asked to collaborate on research with colleagues in psychology, sociology, English, or nursing and other health fields. It is even easier to get grants if we present our collaboration across the fields. Why should we separate ourselves even within our own literacy field? Why can't we be flexible and open to each other and mingle our knowledge and discourse for the benefit of the people and the nation we serve? James Gee (1996) states: "Academicism, in its drive for specialization, too often encourages a narrow focus on bits and pieces of the sorts of coordinations I have named Discourses" (190).

Literacy Education for New Immigrant ESL Students (or Minority Children)

Before Alice came to IS 131, the teaching in ESL classes was very skills-based, as I showed with a seventh-grade lesson on practicing writing the letters *A* and *B*. The lessons were organized according to the language skills taught, in which grammar and spelling were the main content of instruction. Textbooks and worksheets were the learning materials. When we first promoted using trade books and the writing process approach to the teaching of new immigrant ESL students in IS 131, we were confronted with resistance with the statements like "These children need skill drills," and "They can't read and write without mastering the basic skills."

Throughout this book, I show how the teachers at IS 131 taught the new immigrant students with trade books and real writing to develop their literacy, content knowledge, and language skills. As a result, our students in IS 131 are inspired and invited to voice their personal connections, reveal their real emotions, and express their opinions and concerns. Through this kind of meaningful reading and writing, our new immigrant students build content knowledge and develop English language skills. We are helping our students learn to listen, speak, read, and write for communicative purposes as well as for language development goals. In the process of their development as English readers, writers, and speakers, they are given opportunities, specific guidance and instructions, and various strategies in their literacy study. With this progressive approach, our new immigrant ESL students are making steady progress in their literacy and language learning.

No doubt, we are using a progressive model to educate our new immigrant students, who have limited English proficiency and lack cultural and content knowledge for American schools. Many educators in the country have been questioning the progressive approach for educating ESL and minority students. Lisa Delpit's (1988) article "The Silenced Dialogue" has been used as the theoretical backbone for their objection to progressive education for minority children, and the current stress on "back to basics" and "scientific approaches" in the nation has given much support for skills-based instruction for minority students and children of color.

I am very much concerned with the advocacy of isolated skills-based instruction for ESL students, minority students, or children of color. Delpit's (1988) criticism of the writing process paradigm and liberal educators in general in her article has misled many people to interpret her article as a call for the skills approach and scripted programs for nonmainstream students or children of color, though she repeatedly stressed "students must be taught the codes needed to participate fully in the mainstream of American life, not by being forced to attend to hollow, inane, decontextualized subskills, but rather within the context of meaningful communicative endeavors" (43) and specifically stated that "actual writing for real audiences and real purposes is a vital element in helping students to understand that they have an important voice in their own learning process" (33). I believe that Delpit was and still is heard only partially and used as a defense or an advocate for directed instruction (another term for skills-based teaching) for ESL, minority, and struggling students and children of color. Not long ago, I heard a colleague, when talking about a scripted reading program, say, "I won't use it for my own children, but for those children [of color in a poverty school], they need this," because it provides a structured way of learning basic skills. This kind of talk is not uncommon among educators.

In describing what and how the teachers have taught specifically, and what the new immigrant students have achieved in their literacy and language learning in IS 131 in this book, I have demonstrated that we can use trade books and teach real writing to develop the students' language skills for ESL and minority students. Our teachers provide explicit instruction and teach the codes and knowledge that the students need to participate in mainstream American society. In teaching writing, our teachers use the process approach to help students produce quality products and develop their language skills through integrating reading, writing, and theme-inquiry activities. In teaching, our teachers don't need textbooks or worksheets to direct them on what and how to teach. They teach according to what individual students need. They are constantly giving their students explicit instruction through minilessons, individual conferences, and small-group teaching on skills and content explanation without relying on predesigned programs.

Process writing, a model of progressive education in teaching writing, was, and still is, misinterpreted as only stressing process but neglecting product and promoting peer response or a learning community but not providing explicit instruction. This misinterpretation results from poor practice, which may be the consequence of mandate changes or a lack of sufficient staff development or support for teachers. Any poor teaching tends to hurt most the students who are struggling to learn for various reasons, among whom are ESL learners, minority students, new immigrants, and children of color.

I agree that ESL and some nonmainstream students do need more explicit instruction. Some worksheets and language drills may be necessary. But they also need whatever is good for mainstream students, such as reading aloud, interactive learning, inquiry projects, book talks, reading response journals, and writer's notebooks. This kind of teaching stimulates students to learn, and the students who struggle to learn need even more stimulation and personal connection. Our new immigrant students in IS 131 proved that they have much to say and are able to find ways to express themselves. In IS 131, rather than adopting any scripted program, the school provided its teachers with sufficient staff development and support to help them improve their teaching for the newly arrived immigrant students. In sum, our work in IS 131 has proved that our new immigrant students have benefited from progressive education, and progressive education is not just for middle- or upper-class white mainstream students when it is practiced properly.

The Image of "Model Minority"

The Chinese students I have discussed in this book don't fit the image or the stereotype of "model minority." I used to enjoy this image, feeling proud and flattered, and also internalized it until I came to know the new Chinese immigrant children in New York's Chinatown. My study of the Chinatown new immigrants has made me realize that this "model minority" image over-generalizes one group of people for the whole race. And among Asians, there are so many different nationalities with vast differences in culture, history, religion, language, and geography. As Chinese, we never think we are the same as each other and, in fact, Chinese immigrants in Chinatown differ in many ways. Asians make up almost half of the world's population. If this "model minority" image were true, then half of the world population should be high achievers. The percentage of illiteracy in many Asian countries, including China, is much higher than that in the European countries. According to a report presented at an international conference on literacy, by 1995, there were 145 million people that remained illiterate in China because of high dropout rates in middle and high schools (Popkins 2000).

This stereotype is harmful to both high-achieving and other Asian students. The high achievers, who make up only a small percentage of the whole ethnic group, feel they must live up to this image and work as "nerds" to get to the top. Competition drives them. To be better than others is the primary goal in their lives. A son of a friend of mine has suffered a mental breakdown because he could not tolerate being number two or three in class, and even in tennis, if he cannot be number one, he refuses to play. Now his mother says, "I care about nothing, as long as he can be happy." A daughter of another friend recently committed suicide when she didn't receive a scholarship as she had anticipated.

This stereotype hurts more of the Asian students who are not high achievers at school. They are ashamed of themselves, as they are not supposed to have any problems in learning. Stacey Lee's (1996) study reports that struggling Asian students refuse to ask for help when they need it, as they don't want people to think that they are not like the other Asians. They blame themselves for not rising to their image. They either pretend that they are okay or withdraw themselves socially. On the other hand, teachers tend not to pay much attention to them, as those students appear occupied—not causing troubles but following directions—until they fall too far behind. And the parents of the struggling students are very frustrated, as they feel they have totally failed in educating their children. They either blame themselves or think that their children are either lazy or genetically incompetent rather than seeking help or looking for causes that are preventing their children from achieving success.

There are so many studies concerning the education of African Americans and Hispanic Americans, but few on educating Asian Americans because Asian students are only associated with the high-achieving image. As a result, those students who need a lot of help, like the large percentage of our students in Chinatown schools, receive little notice or assistance nationwide. At the New York State Conference on Bilingual Education held in spring 2001, the issues discussed had little to do with the Chinese student population, which makes up 11 percent of the student population in New York, and quite a large percentage of those fail to pass the standardized tests required by the state.

Worst of all, the stereotype of Asians as the "model minority" has caused tension and splits among ethnic minority groups. This stereotype implies that if one minority group can do well despite the discrimination and prejudice they have experienced, or cultural and language barriers they have encountered, then other minority groups should be blamed for their failure, and not society or people who openly or subtly practice prejudice. Furthermore, this stereotype has not only silenced Asian Americans and prevented them from joining civil rights groups to fight for their rights but also intensified interracial competition and conflicts. The Los Angeles burning and New York subway shooting incidents in which one minority burned and killed other minorities are the consequence of this intensification among minority groups. When Dr. Martin Luther King gave his famous "I Have a Dream" speech, he pleaded for equal rights for all, and had on his mind all the ethnic minority people that had been suppressed, not just blacks or one certain ethnic group. If he were alive and saw Los Angeles burning, his heart would sink even deeper.

The newly arrived Chinese immigrants encounter the same difficulties as those experienced by the Mexican migrant workers (as a matter of fact, many Chinese come into the country via the same route as the Mexicans at the Mexican borders). The Chinese immigrant children in New York Chinatown experience struggles at school and poverty in life just as the children of the Mexican immigrant workers. What has made us who we are is much more complicated than a race, a culture, or a country that people share and from which they are originated. Any stereotype, whether positive or negative, prevents us from recognizing and accepting individuality.

Parental Involvement—A Cultural-Bound Perception

Parental involvement is crucial for the children's school performance. But the parents of most Chinatown new immigrant students are not able to be as involved with their children's education as we desire. Many Chinese believe that the best way to help their children's education is to manage to send them to a good school. Those parents feel they have done that once they put their children in an American school, as they believe America is a better society than China, so logically its schools will also be better. Once they put their children in a good school, then it is the task of teachers to educate them, not the parents. They respect teachers as professionals who should know better than they about how to educate their children. Volunteering in the school, assisting on

If only non-immigrant Americans felt this way!! what a better perception teaching would recieve!

a field trip, or corresponding with the teachers regularly about their children's education may sound strange or even be seen as intrusive in the eyes of many Chinese parents.

The parents of our new immigrant students work day in and day out to provide their families with food, shelter, and a stable life, and perhaps a possibility for a good future. This is considered as the most these parents can do for their children and their families. They see their role in their children's education as making sure their children listen to the teachers, follow the teachers' directions, and do their homework. In this country, it is hard for them even to fulfill this role, as making ends meet takes all their energy and time. In addition, they feel that they're less adequate to help their children, as they don't know much English.

America is a print-literate society. We expect parents to read to their children and to help them with their homework. Most of our students' parents rarely saw their parents read or write, and they were never read to while growing up. This kind of parental involvement may sound very strange to them. I grew up in a very literate family in China, with two parents who were professional writers and a home filled with books. But I don't remember my parents ever reading to me. They checked my homework once in a while and only showed interest in the grades I received. But I knew if a teacher called home, I would be grounded for days.

I do believe parental involvement plays an important part in our children's education. But we have to know different cultures value different ways to support their children's education. Most of the new Chinese immigrants in Chinatown don't have time to volunteer at school, don't know how to help, and don't feel adequate assisting their children with their schoolwork. If we interpret their little involvement with the school as not caring, then why would they care enough to bring their children to this country for an education that they think is much better than that in China? The most recent story I have heard from the students and Chinatown residents about the new Chinese immigrants is that fathers bring their children to this country and leave their wives in China because it is very hard to get visas for the entire family. In order not to delay their children's education in the United States, many couples prefer to be physically separated themselves rather than to leave their children in China. This separation could last ten to fifteen years, or even longer. This shows that their children's educational welfare is the priority of their emigration. For this goal, they are willing to sacrifice nearly everything. How many families or husbands and wives in this country are willing to be separated for years in order for their children to receive an education that they think would benefit their children's future? To Chinese parents, their biggest involvement with their children's education is providing them an opportunity that may lead them to a good future. But to many Americans, the sacrifice these families have made for their children's education may sound inhumane or detrimental to the family structure. Here lies a cultural difference in the concept of family values. It has been a long tradition (for centuries) in China that men (now women too) leave their families (parents, spouses, and children) to go to a faraway land for education or fortune making. For the Chinese, to maintain a sense of family structure means that someone in the family has to sacrifice the present to make sure the family can survive and be prosperous from generation to generation. In this sense, these immigrant parents have done more than what most American parents would do for a good education for their children.

Literacy Standard for New Immigrant Children

Most of the new Chinatown immigrant children are not high achievers and cannot meet the standard set for the students at the same grade in this country. They are behind the other students of their age in this country in addition to the different barriers they encounter in the new culture. From the student writing cited in the chapters, we can tell that even though their writing shows a great progress in their literacy and English language development, their English language skills are still far below the standard of the grade at which they are placed. As John, a seventh-grade ESL teacher in IS 131, said, the teachers' goal for their English language beginners is to raise their English language ability from zero to the second grade within a year. That is a huge jump for those learners, which is also shown through reading tests given by the state, but they are still years behind the grade-level requirement. Anyhow, regardless of how hard the teachers and these students work in IS 131, they encounter numerous difficulties in meeting the grade standard. The policy in New York State for assessing the literacy achievement of new immigrant students is that after three years in this country, they will be assessed with the same measurement as anyone else. Many of the students in IS 131 are struggling with this standard requirement, and the teachers and administrators are pressured to help their students meet the standard. As Ourania stated, sometimes they have to teach for the test, though they don't feel right doing so.

I am very concerned with the current overwhelming stress on high-stakes testing starting from the third grade up in this country, especially with the normed assessment for all students despite their very diverse backgrounds. IS 131, which can't hide itself on the island, is heavily affected by this crisis in education. Most of our new immigrant students made a leap in their literacy learning within a year at school, but since the progress was hard to show through normed assessment, the school was put on corrective action by the state. Alice and her teachers had to make sure to raise their test scores within a certain time limit. One day two years ago, I walked into the office, which was stacked with testing preparation booklets, and saw all the paraprofessionals busy counting and stamping them one by one, where they usually categorized and registered the newly purchased literature books. Alice and Pam said to me, "It is depressing, but we have to pay our attention to those tests, or we may lose our school." Under the tremendous pressure of high-stakes testing sweeping the nation, we must squander valuable teaching time for test preparation. For the new immigrant students who have much to make up in order to continue their education in this country, teaching time is too precious to waste on something that we all know won't help them much with their literacy development and transition into our culture.

What exactly is our goal in educating these new immigrant children? Their parents trust us; they also trust our educational system and that the American schools will prepare their children for this world. We are teaching these new immigrant students English language skills, knowledge, and concepts that are needed not just for middle school or going to high school or passing standardized tests but also to help them transition to, adapt to, and love this country. In order to love this country, they first have to love themselves, to understand why they have had to give up so much in return for the life in this land, and to see the beauty of this country. Ultimately, they can truly feel free: free to be able to do anything and be *anyone* in this new world, which, after all, is their American dream.

Some of our students may never pass standardized tests at their grade level because of the barriers they face at school and in their new lives. But we can still, as the faculty in IS 131 is doing, help our students to learn and achieve as much as they can. For the benefit of these students, the mandated curriculum and standards can't control our teaching. If we help our students build confidence in learning and see the beauty and values of this nation, then they will become motivated to learn as much as they can while they are in school and, we hope, to continue their interest in learning for their entire lives. If they are confident about themselves as readers, writers, and learners, they will not stop learning for the rest of their lives. Unlike China, in America there is no age limit in receiving education. As long as one has the desire to learn, opportunity for advancing one's education is always available. In helping these new immigrant children, our educational goal for them should be to build their competence, confidence, and knowledge when they are at school, so they are able to continue their learning throughout their lives.

But if we teach to cover curriculum and to help students pass standardized tests, we will damage them badly. Most of the Chinatown new immigrant students' parents were victims of standardized tests in China. They had no

way to go on to college or even to high school in China. That is why they up-
rooted their families and risked their lives to come to this country. Their children are confronted with more barriers and difficulties in the schools of
America than they were in China. If we overemphasize testing here, they will
be doomed. How can they feel good about themselves if they fail tests all the
time? How can they see hope for their future? How can they perceive America
as a better place for them than China? They will become laden with their loss,
pain, and alienation. In order to give these students a chance, we sometimes
have to forget about tests and ignore the curriculum requirement and start
where they are. Then we will see what they can do and constantly push them
to their next level. Standardized tests are said to offer accountability for our
teaching, but what affects our students' learning and our teaching is multi-
faceted and often out of our control. We have no control over where to place
our students, no control over their educational backgrounds, and no control
over their birthplace, but we *can* have control over how to educate them and
how to help them progress and gain confidence as learners if we are given
control over our teaching.

We have to challenge our students where they are in their learning process.
Teaching for tests is to ignore the students individually and how they learn.
To challenge our students is to push them to their next level, to broaden them,
to enrich them, and to introduce them to new territories. The faculty, administrators, and staff in Chinatown schools, despite all the pressure from high-
stakes testing, never stop thinking of what more we can do to improve the
education and the lives of these new immigrant children.

References

Atwell, N. 1998. *In the Middle: New Understandings About Writing, Reading, and Learning.* 2d ed. Portsmouth, NH: Heinemann.

Barbieri, M. 2002. *"Change My Life Forever": Giving Voice to English–Language Learners.* Portsmouth, NH: Heinemann.

Calkins, L. 1995. *The Art of Teaching Writing.* 2d ed. Portsmouth, NH: Heinemann.

Chomsky, N. 1990. Lecture. March, Manchester, NH.

Crawford, J. 1991. *Bilingual Education: History, Politics, Theory and Practice.* Los Angeles: Bilingual Educational Services.

Cummins, J. 1986. "Empowering Minority Students: A Framework for Intervention." *Harvard Educational Review* 56 (1): 18–36.

Delpit, L. 1988. "The Silenced Dialogue: Power and Pedagogy in Educating Other People's Children." *Harvard Educational Review* 5 (3): 280–98.

Freeman, D., and Y. Freeman. 1994. *Between Worlds: Access to Second Language Acquisition.* Portsmouth, NH: Heinemann.

——— 1998. *ESL/EFL Teaching: Principles for Success.* Portsmouth, NH: Heinemann.

Gee, J. 1996. *Social Linguistics and Literacies: Ideology in Discources.* 2d ed. New York: Routledge, Falmer, Taylor, and Francis.

Goodman, K. 1994. Lecture. May 19, Towson, MD.

Graves, D. L. 1995. *A Fresh Look at Writing.* Portsmouth, NH: Heinemann.

——— 2002. *Testing Is Not Teaching: What Should Count in Education.* Portsmouth, NH: Heinemann.

Harvey, S. 1998. *Nonfiction Matters: Reading, Writing, and Research in Grades 3–8.* Portland, ME: Stenhouse.

Harwayne, S. 2001. *Writing Through Childhood: Rethinking Process and Practice.* Portsmouth, NH: Heinemann.

Heard, G. 1989. *For the Good of the Earth and Sun: Teaching Poetry.* Portsmouth, NH: Heinemann.

Heath, S. B. 1983. *Ways with Words: Language, Life and Work in Communities and Classrooms.* New York: Cambridge University Press.

Howard, J. 2001. "Inside Chinese classrooms." *Reading Today* (June/July): 4.

Keene, E. O., and S. Zimmerman. 1997. *Mosaic of Thought: Teaching Comprehension in a Reader's Workshop.* Portsmouth, NH: Heinemann.

Kinkead, Gwen. 1992. *Chinatown: A Portrait of a Closed Society.* New York: Harper/Collins.

Krashen, S. D. 1991. *Bilingual Education: A Focus on Current Research.* Washington, DC: National Clearinghouse for Bilingual Education.

——— 1996. *Under Attack.* Culver City, CA: Language Education Association.

——— 1999. *Condemned Without a Trial: Bogus Arguments Against Bilingual Education.* Portsmouth, NH: Heinemann.

Kwong, P. 1987. *The New Chinatown.* New York: Hill and Wang.

Lee, S. J. 1996. *Unraveling the "Model Minority" Stereotype.* New York: Teachers College Press.

New York City Department of Education. 2002. *www.nycenet.edu*

Olson, D. R. 1994. *The World on Paper.* London: Cambridge University Press.

Popkins, J. 2000. Literacy in China. Presentation at Nepal and Livelihoods Conference, 4–7 December, Kathmandu, Nepal.

Rief, L. 1991. *Seeking Diversity: Language Arts with Adolescents.* Portsmouth, NH: Heinemann.

Romano, T. 2000. *Blending Genre, Altering Style: Writing Multigenre Papers.* Portsmouth, NH: Heinemann.

Sachs, S. 2001. "Within Chinatown: A Slice of Another China." *The New York Times,* 22 July, pp. 26–28.

Shaughnessy, M. P. 1977. *Errors and Expectations.* London: Oxford University Press.

Thomas, W. P., and V. P. Collier. 1998. "Two Languages Are Better Than One." *Educational Leadership* 55 (4): 23–26.

Vygotsky, L. S. 1978. *Mind in Society.* Edited by M. Cole et al. Boston, MA: Harvard University Press.

Wong, B. P. 1982. *Chinatown: Economic Adaptation and Ethnic Identity of the Chinese.* Chicago: Holt, Rinehart, and Winston.

Xie, Y. 2001. Recent Development of Satellite TV Normal Education in China. Presentation at the National Laboratory School Association. July, Gainesville, FL.

Index